Praise for *Standing for Reason*

"John Sexton has been a remarkable university president. The enlightened pages of this book are a product of his thought, experience, and, above all, his passion about the future of universities."
—**Robert Berdahl,** former president of the University of Texas at Austin, the University of California, Berkeley, and the Association of American Universities

"Both a memoir of the heart and a call to action of the mind, *Standing for Reason* vividly reimagines the American university in an era of rising anti-intellectual fervor and the triumph of absolutism over thought. John Sexton, the uniquely passionate teacher who led NYU to the top ranks of the world's universities, has delivered a must-heed lesson plan for higher education."
—**Arthur Browne,** author and former editor in chief, *New York Daily News*

"In this remarkable book, John Sexton argues that our nation must reclaim the public purposes of higher education. In doing so, he offers a vision of excellence and inclusion that captures the essence, mission, and potential of the twenty-first-century university. This book provides a beautifully reasoned manifesto for the value proposition that a quality education is an investment, not an expense, one that every nation, especially America, must afford if we are to create a better world for all. John calls upon us to combat the 'marginalization of seriousness' and to create a shared global commitment to educational quality for all. And he shows us how this can be done."
—**Martha Kanter,** executive director, College Promise Campaign, and former under secretary, U.S. Department of Education

"At a time when higher education and its values are under attack from a broad array of critics, from right-wing legislators wielding budget axes to student activists trying to shut down speakers with opposing views, John Sexton is a sorely needed voice for the idea of liberal arts, research, and independent scholarship. Agree with him or not—and consistent with his fifty-year career from high school debate coach to global university president, he makes us think—*Standing for Reason* could not have arrived at a more critical moment."

—**Gara LaMarche,** president, Democracy Alliance

"John Sexton, one of America's best known and most accomplished university leaders, helped transform NYU from what was forty years ago a regional university, struggling to survive, into one of the best and most important universities in the world. In his latest book, he asks how universities can help heal the anger and polarization that have become central features of America's civic culture, and he provides a detailed and compelling answer: Universities must recommit themselves to be centers of open, robust, and even controversial debate, and, by doing so, foster the development of a more informed and collaborative community; they must expand their global reach, as NYU has done with its global network and its new campuses in Abu Dhabi and Shanghai; and, working with government, they must expand access to high-quality higher education for all students. His arguments are thoughtful, carefully examined, and persuasive. If we have the energy and commitment to implement his plans, our universities will lead the way in embracing differences, dialogue, and understanding in a way that our interconnected society desperately needs.

—**Ted Mitchell,** president, American Council on Education

"John Sexton, who so ingeniously redefined theological saves and errors in his *Baseball as a Road to God*, now gives us his latest book, *Standing for Reason*, in which he argues convincingly that global universities are the last, best sanctuaries for civic and civil discourse and the best incubators for equal opportunity in an ecumenical world. If he can do for global education and equal opportunity what he accomplished for New York University, the world will be a better and fairer place."
—**Sam Roberts,** *New York Times*

"*Standing for Reason* stands for more than that: It stands for the values of an open mind, of rigorous debate, and helps define the role that colleges and universities can play in a world where knowledge is both created and destroyed with each passing day. John Sexton, in lucid prose, explores the ways the hardening dogmatism of the twenty-first century has led not only to the calcification of opinion but to the increasing substitution of fiction for fact. He calls this phenomenon the rise of secular dogmatism. While he skillfully diagnoses this ill, he also reminds us that the beauty of higher education is that it underpins our ability to push back against dogmatism with reason. There is, in fact, progress to be made in the world, and sustaining it is up to each of us."
—**Gabrielle Starr,** president and professor of English and neuroscience, Pomona College

"John Sexton has been teaching, and thinking about teaching, for almost sixty years, and yet he remains young, that is, passionately engaged, open-minded, and original. When he writes of the 'secular dogmatism' that afflicts our age, he does so through vivid memories of his own liberation from dogma at his Jesuit high school. When he insists that it is the university's highest calling to serve as a 'sacred space' for reasoned discourse, he speaks with the authority of a professor, a dean, and perhaps the most transformative university president of the last generation. When he lays out a vision for the 'global network university' of the future, it is today's New York University, and his own handiwork as president, that he is describing. Sexton has, in short, a hard-earned authority on the great questions of higher education that literally no one else can match."

—**James Traub,** journalist, *New York Times* and *Foreign Policy*, and author of several books, most recently *John Quincy Adams: Militant Spirit*

Standing for Reason

Standing for Reason

The University in a Dogmatic Age

JOHN SEXTON

FOREWORD BY GORDON BROWN

Yale UNIVERSITY PRESS

New Haven and London

Yale University Press books may be purchased in quantity for educational, business, or promotional use. For information, please e-mail sales.press@yale.edu (U.S. office) or sales@yaleup.co.uk (U.K. office).

Set in Minion type by IDS Infotech Ltd.
Printed in the United States of America.

Library of Congress Control Number: 2018960094
ISBN 978-0-300-24337-6 (hardcover : alk. paper)

A catalogue record for this book is available from the British Library.

This paper meets the requirements of ANSI/NISO Z39.48-1992 (Permanence of Paper).

10 9 8 7 6 5 4 3 2 1

For Lisa, who formed our world, and
for Jed, Katie, Danielle, Julia, Ava, and Natalie, who sustain it

Contents

Foreword

Gordon Brown

Former Prime Minister of the United Kingdom, and
United Nations Special Envoy for Global Education

John Sexton's book is important, and it is timely. In *Standing for Reason*, one of the world's most celebrated university presidents—well-known not just on one continent but on all continents—highlights the dangers of a post-truth world where facts and assertion are equated, where the public's confidence in the fundamental institutions of government and society is at an all-time low, and where we are witnessing, in an increasingly pervasive way, the devaluation of thought itself.

In this insightful analysis, John describes these trends, but he does not stop there. He goes on to outline a role for our universities in countering them, and he offers a vision of a new form of university, one pioneered under his leadership—and, if the policy proposals he offers are made law, one that truly will be available to all who deserve it. In doing so, he gives our fragmented world a much-needed message of hope.

Forty years ago, I was, like John, a university lecturer. I spoke of how our great universities stood for objectivity, impartiality, rationality, the pursuit of truth, the search for knowledge, the defence of reason. Years later I joked that these are the qualities I had to leave behind when I went into politics. Little did I know, when I started using that joke, that in the course of my lifetime these values that are central to a free, democratic society would be so threatened that my joke would become a call to action. The active defence of these values is now an essential mission for all thinking citizens.

We are experiencing the growth of what John brilliantly calls "secular dogmatism." "What we have seen is a marginalization of seriousness," he writes. "What we need instead is a marginalization of dogmatism." Standing up to dogmatism has become the challenge of our age.

John's credentials for writing about this new world go beyond his nearly three decades as a university leader in America's most international city. He started his teaching life as a prize-winning debate coach, devoting his twenties and thirties to transforming the prospects of young students, from the often-unconfident adolescents they were into the mature, rounded, and successful people he knew they could become.

After studying law at Harvard, he became a law professor at, and then dean of, the New York University School of Law. Under his leadership, the law school came to be a world leader, one that shaped how other law schools defined themselves.

Then, after being thrust not by choice but by what was effectively conscription into the position of NYU's president, he elevated that university into a world-renowned institution— creating the first global network university, with comprehensive "portal" campuses in Abu Dhabi and Shanghai and twelve other study centres on six continents. This new version of what a university can be, which already has become a beacon for attracting talented faculty and students, foreshadows the interconnected, secularly ecumenical world (a "community of communities") that he describes and hopes will be.

John has done more than any other university president in recent times to encourage universities to think globally. So when in the UK our government set up a review of how American and British universities could cooperate more closely in our new global economy, he was the natural and obvious American to chair the enquiry. A decade ago, in the report that was produced, he and a diverse group of university leaders offered the seeds of a worldview that is, in this book, fully developed.

In these pages, John makes the case for rational argument and what he calls "dialogic dialogue." Ideally, as he argues, everyone would begin with a body of commonly accepted facts and openly discuss their implications for policy. The starting point of John's prescription is his call for a conversation in which everything is on the table—what we debate and the way we debate it—and this, he says, can start within our universities.

This, however, is not our world. Today, the public derives more information from social media websites than from all of the major newspaper outlets taken together. One need not believe that the information provided by newspapers is perfectly accurate (no public figure would accept that claim) to see that such a reliance on untested, often anonymous, information is a problem. Here John's thinking is in line with that of George Orwell, who wrote that, "the further a society drifts from the truth, the more it will hate those who speak it." Moreover, as John notes, the public's attention span is shrinking, and the polarisation of our politics has led to a coarsening of debate.

Why have we come to this point at this moment in history? In part, it is because globalisation—in which global sourcing of goods and global flows of capital have replaced national ones—now appears to many as a runaway train that is out of control and uncontrollable. The world looks leaderless, and globalisation itself lacks a human face, other than the faces of its victims. Indeed, for millions who feel left out and left behind, the very term "globalisation" has become a dirty word.

Economic discontent has bred political alienation, and many no longer look for politicians to offer alternatives. Instead, they call upon them to articulate their anger—hence the attractions of a post-truth politics.

But, as John writes, the modern phenomenon of globalisation involves much more than its economic manifestation. While a version of it can drive people into silos and inward-looking isolationism, a more positive version can be a catalyst for what he sees as a "transformative cultural and societal change that touches the range of human experience, forcing us into relationships with people beyond our borders in unprecedented ways."

Centuries ago, human beings moved from a tribal world that was for millennia inward-looking to a "divergent" one, where individual identity became paramount and communities formed into nations. Today, the logic of globalisation can be seen as pointing to a further shift—a positive one—this time to a "convergent" world, where the people of the world come together to create a community of communities, independent and interdependent at the same time—in short, an advance in how we humans populate the world. As John puts it: "The great question of our time is how peoples around the world will respond to global compression and the inclusion of unfamiliar elements, drawn invisibly from other cultures, into so many aspects of their familiar, local environment." He adds, perceptively: "By hunkering down for a battle against the forces of change, those who choose this path will only hasten what some predict will be a 'clash of civilizations.'"

The fear is that globalisation's centrifugal forces will destroy local identities. This cultural concern about globalisation has been all too apparent in America and Europe. But, John contends, greater interconnectivity need not destroy our diversity. "It is up to us," he writes, "whether globalisation incorporates and celebrates the wonder of difference, maximising its benefits while minimising its costs."

Here John draws from a wealth of personal experience—practical evidence from his own effort to create NYU Abu Dhabi, NYU Shanghai, and NYU's global network. He cites the example of how in NYU Abu Dhabi, young people from all over the world and from every social class—chosen by merit—have blended into one vibrant community, even as each honours and lives his or her own heritage. That this community of roughly fifteen hundred students from over 125 countries, joined by faculty and staff from six continents, thrives in the midst of all the tensions posed by migration, dislocation, poverty, and terrorism is testimony that there is a way to forge global community without losing individual identity.

"We—humankind—are at an inflection point, a critical threshold," John writes. He warns that we soon must choose between the fear that is the currency of populism and the hope that is at the core of what he calls "the second axial age." In doing so, he says we must navigate between two alternatives: the Scylla of chauvinism and the Charybdis of unbounded pluralism.

And here the role of universities is pivotal. Universities have survived where other ancient institutions have collapsed—indeed, of the eighty-five institutions that exist today as they did five hundred years ago, seventy are universities—and they endure because they are directed by responsible global citizens who have guarded freedom of enquiry. As they are called upon to play a role both in elevating public discourse and in shaping globalisation for the good, they must articulate clearly—and adhere steadfastly to—their core principles. But, as individuals at universities describe those principles, they must take care to listen to the arguments of others—prepared to think anew about what has been too often taken for granted and ready to test established ideas in new contexts.

This book's proposals for dealing with what John calls the long arc of globalisation are not just bold but original and start with reform within the universities themselves. Universities should develop what might ultimately become a "universal declaration of core principles," promoting the very rational thinking that has all too often been swept aside. And they "must marshal our academic and then our political leaders to press the agenda of discourse, disseminating into public life the standards and habits of inquiry so central to campuses at their best."

Rightly, because he sees no contradiction between excellence and equality of opportunity, he wants universities opened up to all with the talent and desire to use them well. He offers a comprehensive set of proposals to advance this outcome, including an income-contingent system of grants and repayment—what in the UK would take the form of "a graduate tax"—to bring more students from less privileged backgrounds to apply for university without experiencing the fear of spiralling debt. This commitment to inclusion is a crucial element of his thesis, because if universities are to play the central role he posits for them in shaping society, it is imperative that all voices from all sectors of society be heard within their walls.

John's communitarian approach identifies with a tradition expressed most eloquently by what Adam Smith in *The Theory of Moral Sentiments* called the "circles of empathy." Our support for each other, which starts in our families and among close friends, can extend outwards into the larger community, Smith said, in ever-expanding circles of solidarity and, in time, beyond our shores.

John Sexton highlights what Smith prophesied would make us more sympathetic towards our fellow citizens across the globe. We are privy to greater information about others—and generally we are less prejudiced. There is widespread communication across and between societies, so we can understand each other better. And the education of the moral sense of each of us makes it possible to imagine that the global community John discovers in universities can extend more broadly across the world. It is for these reasons that John can now envisage a world where we can "discover in another tradition values that are submerged or only inchoate in our own."

But his proposals require something else that he has in abundance—optimism about human nature. Writing movingly first in his preface about a great teacher who formed him and then in the conclusion about his beloved wife, Lisa (who died all too young), he returns in the end to his belief in the possibility of "secular ecumenism" as an antidote to "secular dogmatism": if so many could move (as they have) from a religious triumphalism and dogmatism to a religious ecumenism, then surely it is possible for a secular version of the ecumenical spirit to prevail. To this he adds something else he has in abundance. John Sexton appears in these pages as he really is—a thought leader, a humanitarian, and an optimist, and also a man of faith. "The only way to have hope is to have faith," he says. "It is out of that faith that I choose to be an optimist."

Preface
Charlie Sent Me

The path that brings me to this book is as serpentine as the most twisted street in Greenwich Village, home of New York University. Village aficionados delight in the confusion of tourists or uptowners (those very different New Yorkers who live above 14th Street) when they reach the corner where West 10th crosses West 4th (instead of running parallel to it). At that spot, they ask with bewilderment: "Where do I go?" For me, as I try to set the context for the views expressed here, the question is: "Where do I begin?"

Let me start with Charlie. Most who are blessed with some success in their lives, or, even more, with joyful and fulfilling lives, can point to a person along the way who shaped the course they took. For me, that person is Charlie, whom I first met as I entered an extraordinary Jesuit high school in Brooklyn, where he, fresh from doctoral studies at Columbia, was teaching. It was 1955.

Charlie Winans was a striking presence who could not be missed even in the most crowded room. He was a large man, with prematurely white hair. When he wore a beard, he was, even at a young age, a double for Colonel Sanders of Kentucky Fried Chicken. Charlie had a deep, resonant voice whose sonorous sounds dwarfed any competition for attention. And he was a self-evidently holy man, in the best sense, who delighted in "living fully the joys of God's creations." It was not unusual for him to attend a play or opera or symphony and to conduct a postmortem of the event over food and drinks until three in the morning, only to attend Mass at six. One of his closest friends once wrote of him: "He had the body of Orson Welles, the voice of James Earl Jones, and the soul of Saint Francis of Assisi."

The Jesuits knew that in Charlie, a layman who would devote his entire life to the vocation of teaching (although he often dated, he never married), they had someone very special. They knew that assigning him to teach only English and history—which he did teach, quite magnificently—would be a mistake. Of course, he should direct plays and coach orators. But beyond all this, they conceived something more suited to the full range of this unique man: They put twelve of us in a class that met with him for an hour a day, five days a week, for three years—and they named the class "Charlie."

From the beginning, we knew this class was exceptional, although we had no idea at all what material would be covered. Our time with him played out on a different plane, as was clear from the first words Charlie uttered on the first day: "Boys, on the first date, find out her IQ. Beauty fades, but the need for conversation never will."

Then, the magical tour began. Remember, this was 1955. Nobody was talking about interdisciplinary courses or Eurocentric worldviews. Nobody, that is, except Charlie. First, with the cave paintings and percussion music, and, ultimately, with Jackson Pollock and Aaron Copland, we worked through the millennia examining simultaneously the history, literature, art, and music of the period.

Like all great teachers, Charlie knew his students. I will always remember one class in particular. We had studied the history of ancient Egypt and read both the Book of the Dead and Shakespeare's *Antony and Cleopatra*. With Egyptian music as a score, Charlie used a projector to display on the classroom wall the Giza pyramids. "Boys," he said, "you will never see these pyramids, because you can't drive to them." He knew our limitations. "But there are pyramids to the south of here you can reach by car. They were built by a great civilization most people don't talk about that much, because the British didn't rob these pyramids to stock their museums." There he was in 1956, talking about the provenance of art.

Charlie had a phrase he used to exhort us to live life fully: "Play another octave of the piano." His explanation was a command: "If there are notes you have not touched, reach out and touch them. If there is a food you have not tasted, if there is music you have not heard, if there is a place you have not seen, if there is a person whose story you do not know, reach out to experience more fully the wonders of creation. Expand your horizons. So long as it is legal and moral, try anything new at least once."

Remember that phrase: "Play another octave of the piano." It is the basis for much of what I have done in my professional life and will say in this book.

Charlie incarnated another lesson that influenced me in profound ways. "Consider teaching, boys. It is the noblest and most fulfilling of all vocations." Those words—and the meaning he gave them—captured me from the moment he uttered them. And for nearly sixty years I have lived their truth.

It was Charlie who introduced me to the world of competitive debate and urged me to pursue debating vigorously. He had nothing to do with the debate program, which was a major activity at the school. Indeed, as the drama coach, he competed with the coach of the debate team for talent. It shows how well he knew me and how he put my interests first that he ushered me out of his orbit.

Debate opened my world in unimaginable ways— intellectual, social, even spiritual. It provided the most formidable element of my education. By my senior year, I was good enough to be named the national champion. This attainment, among other things, caught the attention of another extraordinary educator, Father Timothy Healy, later the remarkable and transformative president of Georgetown but in 1959 a relatively young priest at Fordham who was determined to see Fordham produce Rhodes Scholars. He recruited me with that goal in mind.

My father died during my first year there. For some reason, perhaps motivated by Charlie's call to the vocation of teaching (which I had indulged by coaching our high school debate team in my senior year), or perhaps somehow in reaction to my dad's death, I took the subway to my sister's all-girls, Catholic high school in Brooklyn and offered to start a debating team.[1] I assured the principal that the girls would learn a lot, that they would win the national championship, that they would be better for the experience, and that I would raise the money for the team to attend the top tournaments around the country.

When the principal accepted my offer, she framed the next fifteen years of my life. For the weeks during the school year, I devoted nearly a hundred hours (typically including trips out of town from Thursday afternoon until Sunday evening) to what we came to call "the society." The debate topic occupied only part of our time, especially before and after the tournament season. Copying Charlie, I taught the debaters about history, literature, art, and music. Occasionally, during the summer, we would take several weeks to visit the national parks west of the Mississippi (each trip culminated in the fifteen-mile walk down and up the Grand Canyon's Bright Angel Trail so that we could touch the depth of the canyon); and every summer we would spend evenings at Shakespeare in the Park or the Symphony at Lewisohn Stadium—and, of course, a weekend at Tanglewood with the Boston Symphony.

I am very proud of those years. And I am most proud of those young women, who did win the national championship—five times—and scholarships to college and who went on to be leaders in an array of fields, one serving on a higher education board with me later in life when she became president of Hamilton College.

There is a dark side of the story, however. Father Healy was furious that I was never around campus for his meetings. Since I only rarely attended class, my professors, too, were displeased (in those days, they took attendance). My grades suffered. Any hope of academic honors disappeared. Even as I enjoyed success in my nascent teaching career, I limped to graduation with a GPA I recall as around 2.1 (perhaps it was higher, but it certainly began with a 2).

In April 1963, just a few weeks before graduation, Father Healy stopped me as I was walking across the central campus—heading to a class, no less. "You have disappointed us," he said. "But the Vatican Council is happening, and it is important that we Catholics understand other religions. We're starting a PhD program in religion, and we are going to give you a second chance. You will receive a fellowship to pursue a PhD." Tim Healy was going to pay me to go to school!

At the time, I felt honored. Now, I realize that Father Healy had funding for the program but had not found a sufficient number of students (there were only two of us that first year, although it must be said that the other became a spectacular scholar). As he searched the campus, he had spotted me and, assuming correctly that I was focused on my high school students so completely that I had not made plans for the fall, he pounced—displaying simultaneously his mercy and creativity. Unknowingly, he was continuing a process for me that Charlie had begun: the inculcation of a spirit of openness to, and a delight in, encountering difference. The key elements of the worldview I carry today were set in place.

Viewed in hindsight, the embrace of difference may seem unremarkable. But the world looked very different back then. In the very year we began the first sessions of our course with Charlie, a wonderfully progressive Jesuit, Father Daniel Berrigan, had written on the blackboard four Latin words that captured the teaching of the Catholic Church—my church—at the time: *Extra ecclesiam nulla salus* ("Outside the Church there is no salvation"). When I asked if that meant that my friend Jerry Epstein would not go to heaven, he told me: "Unless you baptize him, he will not go to heaven." Even in 1956, Charlie labeled this view "absurd." Soon Pope John XXIII would call us to an "ecumenical" movement that taught us the importance and the joy of seeing the world not just through the one window we had been given at birth but through the many windows in the many rooms of the great mansion of creation.

I arrived at my first graduate class with attitudes unusual for the time. The first was a latent—indeed, largely unconscious—but genuine interest in and instinct for what I would later learn to call ecumenical thinking. My study of religion—just as the Catholic view of the world was changing—only solidified and enhanced what Charlie had planted in us. The second, which was more fully formed and embedded in my being, was an unreserved, absolute embrace of the vocation of teaching and of Charlie's approach to a life in education, in and out of the classroom.

This combination made me a very atypical doctoral candidate, because I entered with an interest in the subject of our courses but without the commitment first and foremost to a life in the discipline, a commitment most doctoral students take for granted. I visualized myself as having a life in education going forward, but I probably would have defined it much more in terms of my high school students than the discipline I was pursuing. So it was, and happily, that as I finished my course work and it was time for me to move into college and university teaching, my choice as to where to pursue my life as a college professor was shaped principally by what would allow me to continue working with my debaters. I did not engage in a search for a place with more prestige or stronger colleagues in my discipline. I simply looked for a setting where I could find life as a college professor fulfilling.

My first full-time position in higher education was at Saint Francis College in Brooklyn, fondly known as "the small college of big dreams." In Saint Francis I found a place I could love—and still love. For ten years, I delighted in the colleagues and students, many the first in their family to attend college, with whom I was very privileged to work. Saint Francis soon gave me tenure and named me head of the department of religion. Then, with not a hint of resistance from the administration, we effected dramatic changes in the department's offerings, quickly incorporating the ecumenical, less triumphalist thinking of the day. We were teaching not only the Quran, the Bhagavad Gita, and the Analects, but also talking about the "death of God" and the "secular city." In short, we were playing new octaves on the piano.

In 1972, some close friends did "an intervention." They knew I had always wanted to go to law school and that I had "postponed" going so that I could continue my work with my debaters. The time had come, they argued as I turned thirty, for me to move on to my next phase. I knew they were right. I planned to study law at a New York school while continuing to work with the girls in the debating society. On that plan, if we took no freshmen into the debate program, the last of the debaters would graduate from high school the same year that I graduated from law school. Unfortunately, none of the New York schools agreed. My disastrously low college GPA combined with the rest of my unorthodox background did not appeal to the admissions officers, who were unanimous in rejecting me.

Here, good fortune struck. One of my references, Laurence Tribe (today the world's leading constitutional expert, but to me then and now primarily a beloved friend), who had recently been tenured at Harvard, had feared that, if he did not write that he had recommended me to his own school, his letter to the other schools would be devalued. And so he had insisted that I apply to Harvard, even though I wanted to stay in New York. Initially, Harvard joined the New York schools in rejecting me, but when Larry appeared in person to urge his colleagues to reconsider my application, they did. So it was that Harvard was the only school to accept me. The problem was that I could not leave New York for Boston until 1975, and I would not break my commitment to see all of my high school debaters through to graduation. My life changed when Harvard's director of admissions, Molly Geraghty, agreed to place me in the class entering three years later in the fall of 1975. I called her every fall until her death to thank her for that act of confidence in me.

Truly, Harvard changed my life. Most important, I met Lisa Goldberg, my true love. We were married on August 2, 1976, just after completing our first year of law school. My time at

Harvard also introduced me to the wonder of the research university and, in 1981, led me to what would be my academic home for the rest of my life, NYU. I became the law school's dean in 1988 and the university's president in 2001. In 2016, I returned to the faculty as president emeritus.

•

My tale yields some useful lessons. First, failure is not necessarily the end of a story; often, there will be a Tim Healy or Molly Geraghty to offer rehabilitation and even redemption. And second, it is good to remember that there was a time, and for some there still is a time, when it was understood that a life in education was the highest calling. Such beliefs may be viewed as anachronistic or naïve to some.

Apart from these lessons, however, and essential to the views expressed here, the accidentally serpentine path I walked yielded a wider perspective on higher education than the perspective of those who took a straight, more traditional path. A teaching life intensely forged with high school students and shaped by a truly great high school teacher, which then moved through the precincts of a small teaching college to one of the world's great research universities, is a life that benefits from an appreciation of realities, empirical and otherwise, of our educational system that often go unnoticed by those who have experienced only elite institutions.

There are over four thousand accredited institutions of higher education in America—public and private, community college through research university, large and small, secular and faith-based, urban and rural, brick and click, and on and on. Conversations about our universities and colleges tend to focus on eighteen- to twenty-four-year-old "coming-of-age" students, but 40 percent of those enrolled in higher education are "later-life learners"—veterans, single parents, or folks who are moving from one job to another.[2] In other words, our higher education system is a symphony orchestra of offerings. And each section of the orchestra is different from the others and indispensable to the orchestra. This is a strength.

Much of what I will say in the coming chapters will apply most directly to America's research universities. Where that is the case, it is a function of the broader role those universities play in society, because of their intrinsically greater scope, and their greater impact upon us—from the research labs that make advances in medicine to the professional schools that produce our teachers, nurses, doctors, and lawyers. Notwithstanding the great breadth and impact of these institutions, however, it would be unfair and downright wrong to view the research university section of the educational orchestra as superior to the other sections, just as it would be unfair and wrong to view the string section of an orchestra as superior to the brass section. Both are required to perform Beethoven's Ninth.

As I moved through three intense professional experiences—the high school debate team, Saint Francis, NYU—I never viewed one as "better" than the others. They certainly were different from one another. Each has a different purpose (the Jesuits call this a *ratio studiorum*), and each uses different methods. At each stage, I found joy and fulfillment. I have no inclination to rank one experience over the others. And were I to do so, there is no certainty that my time in a research university would occupy the top spot. Indeed, if I were forced to live a life in which I could only do one of the three, I would choose to work with the debaters.

In any case, a choice is not necessary—for me or for anyone. There is joy in each section of the orchestra. In the pages that follow, I hope to explore why that is so and how we can make the orchestra play at its best for as many as possible.

Before moving on, I should note another set of idiosyncrasies that likely shape the views expressed here and the way they should be understood.

First and foremost, to this day my core professional identity is as a faculty member. Throughout my time as dean or president, I continued to teach a full schedule (four or five full courses each academic year) and to write (including a *New York Times* bestseller, *Baseball as a Road to God,* based on a course I offer undergraduates at NYU). Second, I did not seek to become NYU's law dean or president. In each case, I came to the office reluctantly and after urging other candidates on those who would make the selection. Third, over the twenty-eight years I served as dean or president, I declined service on compensated boards, instead devoting external time as chair of associations or institutions that related to NYU's mission, such as the American Council on Education, the Consortium of Independent Colleges and Universities, the Association of American Law Schools, the New York Academy of Sciences, and the Federal Reserve Bank of New York. These varied involvements in the collective enterprise of higher education rewarded me with an overarching view of trends, challenges, opportunities, and strategies I would never have had otherwise.

Finally, throughout these years, I made it very clear that time with my family (including extended time "off the grid" in places like the Grand Canyon) was inviolate and would be preserved against any call. I am pleased to say that my colleagues at NYU honored this need completely, granting me the contemplative time and the replenishment provided by secular sabbatarianism.

Inevitably, the chapters of this book have been influenced by my odd journey, which led to the perspectives I have and the values nourished along the way. I hope the result is a book that provides some fresh ideas or ways of looking at what we in higher education do.

•

When I encountered Charlie Winans and Danny Berrigan in the 1950s, most Americans trusted our leaders and the fundamental institutions of society. Today, that trust is gone. The reasons for this change are complex, and I will offer my own view of the causes. In the process, I will highlight two starkly contrasting trends I have witnessed and lived over the intervening decades.

If after college I, an Irish Catholic, had married an Italian Catholic (let alone an Anglican, a Jew, a Muslim, or an atheist), it would have created consternation in the family. As the words Father Berrigan wrote on the board made clear, we believed that we had been given through grace the one true and unquestionable faith. Six decades later, many Catholics (most notably, Pope Francis) have embraced the ecumenical spirit of Pope John XXIII—and the intellectual and spiritual advance that an openness to the insights of other traditions brings. My own family was way ahead of the curve, thrilled forty years ago when I married Lisa, whom they saw to be the truly wonderful woman she was. They never mentioned that she was Jewish, and they accepted without question our decision to raise our children in the Jewish tradition.

Even as this embrace of encounter and dialogue increasingly has come to characterize religious thought and life, political discourse has moved in exactly the opposite direction. Sixty years ago, politicians, for all their faults—and there were many—shared a sense of a commonweal and worked to advance it, even when that noble work forced an admission of past sins (as the Civil Rights Act and Voting Rights Act illustrate). Neither they nor the results they produced were perfect, but there was room to reason and to work together, at least for the great majority on both sides. Today, there is no such room. A chasm separates two warring tribes, with each side wondering how the "others" could be the way they are—and with each side unwilling to engage in a serious conversation with the other.

Against the backdrop of these two antipodal trends (toward ecumenism on the one hand and toward dogmatism on the other), I offer in these pages an integrated argument in four parts. In chapter 1, "Dogmatism, Complexity, and Civic Discourse," I start with the terrifying proposition that, unless current trends are reversed, the enterprise of thought is in danger, as Americans develop an allergy to nuance and complexity and civic discourse warps into a virulent secular dogmatism. Political positions now have been elevated to the status of doctrinal truths, embedded beliefs that are taken as givens and cannot be questioned; they have been "revealed."

In chapter 2, "The Traditional University as Sacred Space for Discourse," I argue that our colleges and universities are the best hope for curing this disease, and I describe the characteristics they must manifest and the policies that their leaders must embrace if they are to serve this role.

In chapter 3, "A University for an Ecumenical World," I argue that some colleges and universities should move beyond this traditional role to assume a more ambitious office: acting as incubators for a secular ecumenism that not only rejects secular dogmatism but also seeks to build a community of interlocking communities, a whole that is greater than the sum of its parts—a world that today is only a dream.

Finally, in chapter 4, "The Final Ingredient: Meaningful Access for All," I contend that, if higher education is to play these two related roles, it is imperative that every person, without regard to station or financial means, have a meaningful opportunity to attend the college or university that matches his or her talent. The public conversation on this question has suffered from a surplus of misinformation and a shortage of creative ideas. I try to correct the misinformation and to offer a practical, effective, and even politically palatable way forward. The moral point is very simple, however: If we hope to create an ecumenical world, every citizen of that world must have the opportunity to acquire the tools that can be used to shape it. That, in brief, is what lies ahead in these pages.

Now, as Charlie would say: "Onward and upward!"

Standing for Reason

1

Dogmatism, Complexity, and Civic Discourse

Prelude

Over twenty-five years ago, in a speech at Saint Louis University, I focused on a too-little-noticed day in 1957, a turning point in American history: October 8, 1957. The day's edition of New York's major tabloid the *Daily News* bore two screaming headlines. The first announced the demise of the Russian satellite whose launch had shaken American self-confidence to its core: "Report Sputnik on Way Down." The second declared the beginning of the end of an America that trusted its institutions: "It's Final: Dodgers Go to L.A."[1] If the Dodgers could betray the good people of Brooklyn, no institution could be trusted.

A decade ago, a friend, the first in his family to go to college, told me that in the 1950s his father would respond to his youthful questions about issues of the day with a soothing assurance: "Don't worry, son. They're taking care of it for us." We don't say that to our children anymore.

In a way, skepticism about authority is a sign of maturity. The equanimity of the 1950s was built on hidden sins. And "they" were not always at work taking care of it—or at least not *for all* of us, or even for most of us. When that reality finally was unmasked, we were forced to confront our failures and the injustices they spawned. This process has been good for our society—but not good enough. To move beyond the sins of the past, we were called to a collective conversation about the measures required to create a just society worthy of a great and moral people. That conversation was begun, but it was never completed. So, skepticism about authority has metastasized into distrust—distrust of our government, our institutions, our leaders, and even our fellow citizens.

I wish this distrust really could be laid at the doorstep of Walter O'Malley, the devil who moved my Dodgers; if that were so, an easy solution might be at hand. In truth, the causes are more complicated. Over the last three generations, we have lost our sense of the common—a commonweal that binds us in a shared enterprise—and our sense of obligation to each other and to the coming generations. We once viewed our pluralism, at least in principle, as a strength of a welcoming society (*e pluribus unum*); today, many of us openly target our diversity as defining various "others," different from us, who are dangerous.

Over these last sixty years, the world has become miniaturized. Dramatic advances in communication and transportation have shrunk time and space—literally. The very shape of the globe inherently forces a circle of interdependence on issues ranging from migration to climate change. The interdependence of economies is only a small part of it. As the global community confronts this reality, America, where a major harbor features the Statue of Liberty as a symbol of a commitment to pluralism, faces a test of that fundamental premise. No longer protected by the natural isolation created by ocean borders to the east and west, we are not doing well.

We now live in a balkanized society, with understanding in short supply. And this is so because the hard intellectual (and, it must be added, spiritual) work that is the necessary predicate of true understanding is absent. Indeed, just when we most need serious conversation on a range of very tough issues, we, as a society, have developed an allergy to nuance and complexity that devalues thought, knowledge, expertise, and understanding. Many, if not most, of us have retreated into political caves—homes of red and blue "faiths"—in which we are taught about the secular dogmas of our group. We then stand in union with "our people" against "theirs," supporting policies that may be reasonable but certainly not reasoned.

I began to warn my colleagues in the academic world about this trend over two decades ago. Initially, as I played the role of Cassandra, my concern was that, if Americans continued to devalue complex public argument, they would inevitably devalue what our universities do—since the best universities are devoted to exploring complexity as a primary task. There are signs that this diminishment is already happening. A recent survey reported that 58 percent of Republicans say that universities have a negative effect on the way things are going in the country, while just 36 percent say their effect is positive. Only two years ago, these numbers were reversed. The opinions of Democrats, although a bit less negative, are similar.[2]

Our universities are indeed under siege. Still, I hold out hope that they can lead a reversal of the broad societal trend I have described by modeling robust conversation and revealing its benefits. Indeed, I believe universities can play a unique role in rebuilding the kind of discourse on which participatory democracy depends.

We have reached a fateful crossroads: If our universities do not serve as an antidote to the marginalization of seriousness in the public square, they will themselves be marginalized. If demagoguery is rewarded and mendacity becomes the coin of discourse, the lack of faith in society's institutions will become still deeper and more pervasive, until at last society itself will crumble.

Here I Stand

Let me begin by revisiting and expanding upon the elements that inform my views.

I am a person of faith—formed by American Catholicism in the 1950s and transformed by both the Vatican Council of the 1960s and the ideas of progressives like the Jesuit theologian Teilhard de Chardin. I am an unabashed Teilhardian optimist.[3]

I was raised in Brooklyn in the cauldron of Irish-Catholic Democratic politics, at a time when Joseph McCarthy had not yet been revealed as a charlatan and was viewed by many (perhaps even by my mother) as a candidate to join the Heavenly Hosts. The Catholicism instilled in us consisted of a set of simple rules: Avoid meat on Friday, go to Mass on Sunday, and turn away all thoughts of sex until you are married. We were told and believed that this path guaranteed eventual eternal life in heaven, although for most of us the reward would come after a detour to purgatory.

The Second Vatican Council replaced this reductive view of faith with a call to widen our horizons and take up the wonderful burden of personal responsibility. For many of us, this meant wrestling with the moral issues posed by the civil rights movement, the peace movement, and the women's movement—issues that pressed us to confront authority and tradition in ways new to us.

I am also a person of the mind, privileged to have led a research university. My first academic home was in arts and sciences, from my foundational liberal arts education (high school through college), under Jesuits who believed that an inability to read Horace and Homer in Latin and Greek constituted illiteracy, to my time as chair of a college religion department. I then went to law school and, after two years of working for judges, came to New York University and entered the world of the research university. But, as I noted earlier, my résumé does not reveal the most formative influence on my intellectual development—my nearly twenty-year commitment to competitive debate, first as a participant and then as a coach. This experience exposed me, at a remarkably deep level, to the world of ideas and laid the basis for my belief in the centrality of informed dialogue to broader civic discourse.

My worlds—the world of faith and the world of the mind—first came together vividly when, during the Vatican Council, I began my doctoral studies under the direction of an extraordinary Fordham theologian and philosopher named Ewert Cousins. His intellectual journey parallels my own and that of American Catholicism from the 1950s to the decades after Vatican II. Ewert's story must be told.

By 1963, Ewert was a leading expert on the work of Saint Bonaventure, a medieval theologian. Twenty years later, the United Nations celebrated the publication of a twenty-five-volume work on world spirituality for which he was general editor—a magnum opus that explored the world's major faith traditions, exalting their collective insight.

In his later work, Ewert saw our times as nothing less than the dawn of what he called the Second Axial Age, a rare inflection point in human history. In using this term, he invoked a phrase ("Axial Age") coined by philosopher Karl Jaspers about the period from 800 to 200 B.C.E., the era in which, Jaspers argued, humans developed the idea of individuality and came to see themselves as distinct actors.[4]

For Ewert, the Second Axial Age would see the integration of our now fully mature sense of individuality with the collectivity of a new global era. He saw a Teilhardian "planetization"— the reshaping of humanity's intellectual, cultural, and spiritual identity in a global community where, even while maintaining a mature sense of individuality, all would realize a fuller shared destiny (what Teilhard called "Point Omega").

It is a bold vision. Yet, if one compares the Catholic Church of Pope Francis with the Church into which I was born, there has been a radical opening to other traditions, which has been reciprocated as other traditions have joined Catholics in embracing ecumenism. Although there are notable exceptions within and outside Christianity, significant numbers of people from many faiths now display this openness. There is no doubting the possibility of a journey to the world that Pope John XXIII, Teilhard, and Ewert imagined. Among leaders of many of the world's faith traditions, the journey has been made. However, it remains to be seen whether we will seize the possibility of a secular analogue—of a world characterized by secular ecumenism.

The Danger I See

Sadly, even as the last sixty years have seen religious discourse move toward this ecumenical vision, civil discourse has moved in the opposite direction. The mindset that dominated religious discourse as I experienced it decades ago has become a feature of civil discourse, giving birth to what I call pervasive "secular dogmatism." I use the word *dogmatism* here to denote a habit of mind—a close-mindedness, or lack of intellectual open-ness—that is, in this context, completely secular and unrelated to religion.

In his prescient book *The Rhetoric of Reaction* (1991), Albert Hirschman voiced concern over "the massive, stubborn and exasperating otherness of others." He warned that a "systematic lack of communication between groups of citizens, such as liberals and conservatives, progressives and reactionaries," would soon create in the body politic the unsettling condition of "being shut off, not just from opinions, but from the entire life experience of large numbers of one's contemporaries." The result: "As the process feeds on itself, each group will at some point ask about the other, in utter puzzlement and often with mutual revulsion, 'How did they get to be that way?'"[5] Those words describe the contemporary state of our politics.

The chasm between Americans who identify with either political party has widened dramatically. Twenty years ago, 17 percent of Democrats had a "very unfavorable" view of Republicans; today, 55 percent do. Back then, 21 percent of Republicans had that view of Democrats; today, 58 percent do. The median Republican is now more conservative than 92 percent of Democrats, and the median Democrat is more liberal than 94 percent of Republicans. Over 40 percent of those in each party view the other party as a threat to democracy. When asked to describe members of the other party, Democrats and Republicans use the same words: dishonest, immoral, unintelligent, and close-minded.[6]

There are other indicators of this lamentable trend: Sixty years ago, fewer than 5 percent of Americans reported that they would be disturbed if a member of their family married a person who was a member of the other political party; by 2010, 40 percent said they would be unhappy with such an interparty marriage (49 percent of Republicans, and 33 percent of Democrats).[7] The numbers would be even more negative today. One comprehensive study of this data concluded that party polarization exceeds racial polarization.[8] Secular dogmatism has assumed the role of the religious dogmatism of my youth.

The most obvious form of this secular dogmatism can be found in the tendency of some Americans to derive political positions from maxims of religious faith. Mobilized by leaders for whom theology is primarily an instrument of political power, these believers possess a certainty that the word of God reveals correct positions on social issues: God tells us how to vote. Revelation replaces discourse; there is nothing to discuss. The right way to think about issues is received as a secular gift of grace.

It is paradoxical that those who propagate this faith-based politics frequently care less about theology than politics. The allure of political power, of advancing a social agenda through government, is so great that they often are willing to set aside centuries of theological differences to rally together for the cause du jour. Thus, Richard Land, president of the Southern Baptist Ethics and Religious Liberty Commission, was able to say in 2004: "I've got more in common with Pope John Paul II than I do with Jimmy Carter or Bill Clinton"—notwithstanding that Carter and Clinton are lifelong Baptists.[9] And, in 2017, fundamentalist religious leaders could put aside allegations of pedophilia to support an Alabama senatorial candidate, Roy Moore, who embraced their political agenda.

A second and far more pervasive manifestation of secular dogmatism, untethered to any basis in religion, flows directly from the now highly developed allergy to nuance and complexity that I noted earlier, and from a concomitant addiction to simple answers summarized neatly in slogans, untestable by argument in the public square. In the aftermath of the 2016 election, this warning may sound like a critique of that particular election cycle; but the trend toward secular dogmatism was apparent long before anyone viewed Donald Trump as more than a character in tabloid gossip columns and a reality TV star.

In 1996, I first noted the exploitation of the public's growing impatience with the hard work of thought. A political consultant had written a monograph advising clients that the path to electoral victory was not through serious policy discussion, but rather through a sustained attack on lawyers and judges as the causes of our nation's ills. Offering a set of rhetorically "useful" isolated examples, he advised that there would be no cost to the use of extreme, vitriolic language in attacking the stewards and institutions of law. Votes would follow. As he put it: "It's almost impossible to go too far when it comes to demonizing lawyers. . . . You should tap into an anger and frustration with practitioners of law. . . . Attacking lawyers is admittedly a cheap applause line, but it works."[10]

As dean of New York University's School of Law and president of the Association of American Law Schools, I wrote a letter to warn the nation's law deans and professors: "This attack on lawyers is just another version of the attack on judges and the notion of an independent (and sometimes antimajoritarian!) judiciary. And these attacks are part of a larger phenomenon: the tendency of our society to devalue its institutions (whether its government, its universities, or its churches) and to desiccate those who seek to serve them. We are in a time where all too frequently (if not almost always) sloganizing and personal attacks are preferred to engagement on the substance of even (perhaps especially) the most complicated issues."[11]

Today, demagogues mock those who offer complex explanations and answers to vexing problems, and routinely deride the value of expert knowledge. Although superficially our age is

a halcyon era of information and conversation, this very abundance can work against sustaining a public forum populated by
an informed and intellectually curious public. The overwhelming amount of available information presents even the best-read
and most diligent citizen with a serious sorting problem. The
curating function once provided by traditional sources has been
reduced or has disappeared as new, web-based sources see no
premium in applying the standards that once applied to traditional media. Thus, even as technology and social media em-
power many who previously were unheard to become actors in
the drama of public life, they also breed misinformation and
spread falsehoods, diluting the quality of public conversation.
One far-too-common response to this barrage of undifferenti-
ated information is a nihilism that ultimately equates fact with
opinion and reduces argument to bald assertion.

The worldview created by this devolution of thought
is nourished in a feedback loop shaped by what psychologists
call confirmation bias, the tendency to process information
as ratifying what is already believed and to select sources that
reinforce those preexisting beliefs. What was once, for all its
limitations, a canon of information has been supplanted by an
echo chamber, in which too many of our citizens are drawn to
niche channels that mirror their preconceptions. Few are willing to venture beyond the cable news that most clearly caters
to their own worldview.

As our citizens have retreated into news silos, the Fourth
Estate, a traditional *sine qua non* of democracy, has been de-
monized with a previously unimaginable ferocity. Cries of "fake
news" are now heard regularly. And although the tendency
to seek out sources offering congenial views cuts across the
political spectrum, the view that most news is "fake"—that is,
the tendency to dismiss reported stories as untrustworthy—is

concentrated. Roughly 90 percent of Democrats say media criticism keeps politicians from doing things that should not be done; only 40 percent of Republicans say the same. This gap is the widest on the issue since pollsters began asking the question in 1985. As recently as early 2016, the respective numbers were 74 percent and 77 percent.[12]

Moreover, as the gap widens, the attention span of Americans is shrinking. This change is reflected in the increasingly impoverished quality of what our political leaders say in the public forum. What are advertised as candidate debates are in fact only televised opportunities to state and restate simple, preset messages. The "debaters" are coached to avoid addressing the dimensions of the issues or the subtleties of policy, lest they lose their audience. And they avoid discussion of any solutions that, although beneficial in the long run, impose some sacrifice on the voters.

More than ever, we need leaders who will work together to address the dilemmas of our increasingly interdependent and matrixed world, willing to advance policies that call upon the public to pay now for benefits they might not see. The issues we face today are too complicated to be resolved by simple assertions: How do we address the disparity of wealth and opportunity in America—and in the world? How do we provide quality health care at low cost to all citizens? What does it take to reduce the achievement gap in education? What do we do to overcome racism, sexism, and homophobia? How should we treat new immigrants? How do we heal the environment? How do we move from war to peace?

We need as many incisive minds as we can muster to address such problems and the humility to understand that we are more likely to arrive at wise conclusions if we can join forces, knowing that none of us has the entire truth. And yet we have made it far more difficult for our leaders to participate in such discussions. We have created a coliseum culture that reduces public conversation to a set of gladiatorial soundbites.

The growth of secular dogmatism and emergence of a coliseum culture have been exacerbated by the nature of our political system. The structure of America's two-party system creates the likelihood that the shift on an issue of a small number of voters one way or the other can result in huge policy consequences. If red means Republican and blue means Democrat, when American voters cast their ballots they must pick red or blue—even if their own political preferences are purple. When this polarization is the forced choice, Americans divide as close to evenly as can be imagined, by margins of 4 percent or less. The apparently neat division plays out such that the handful (10 to 15 percent) of voters willing to switch across the divide control the outcome of the election.[13]

Whatever the overlapping consensus might be, the fact that the divide in the electorate is so close affects politicians' behavior in critical ways. They speak defensively, worrying about expressing a provocative thought at the wrong time or suffering a slip of the tongue, with cameras ever present to capture the gaffe. Our political conversations are carefully scrubbed, driven by focus-group testing that produces candidates playing the role of scripted salesmen for the product that surveys have shown the public desires.

In this environment, policy makers and candidates state their positions, even in private conversation, in ways that avoid conceding ground. Because compromise can be described by "true believers" as weakness, our putative leaders cannot move to consensus. The result: a decline in honest, open, and probing conversation about public policy solutions to the most confounding issues of the day.

When the consequence of the binary choice is pure red or pure blue, the purest (that is, the most extreme) proponents of red or blue care most intensely about its outcome—and they, the base, come to wield power that is disproportionate. The result is a mutually reinforcing interaction with the secular dogmatism I have described, entrenching and escalating the received political creed.

Finally, when relatively minor shifts in the electorate create potentially seismic shifts in policy by the small margins between victory and defeat, those who maintain power put a very high premium on loyalty. In a bipolar nation, the thought of the reds taking over from the blues, or vice versa, is seen as apocalyptically significant. This emphasis on blind party loyalty breeds the suppression and punishment of internal dissent and the proliferation of litmus tests—a dead weight on the richness of public discourse.

This bipolarity is now a structural component of American political life. The House of Representatives offers a dramatic example, gerrymandered to ensure single-party control of the vast majority of seats. Safe districts, solidly red or blue, yield a House whose members' fealty is to the unshaded hue, with no interest in reaching across the aisle to find common ground. In these safe districts, the real elections occur in the low-turnout party primaries, dominated as it is by the party extremists. In this way, the distance from red to blue grows.

The University as Counterforce

Our great universities can be powerful instruments in reversing the trends I have described. I believe they can incubate and cultivate an open-ended exploration of viewpoints that can be the catalyst for re-creating the public discourse our society needs. And I believe that reasoned debate and nuanced discussion about policies, communicated to an attentive public, can restore trust. But make no mistake about it: It will not be easy, not least because our universities themselves are threatened.

Just as the attention span of Americans has been shrinking, so, too, our society has been losing patience for the slow and sometimes meandering process of refining compelling ideas and the policies that flow from them. Collectively, in part because of our aversion to complexity and in part from our addiction to hyperstimulation in daily life, we have developed an appetite for immediate results and painless solutions. Our nation no longer values planting trees under which others will sit. This kind of thinking does not bode well for the work of universities, which depends on a commitment to the meticulous, unflinching advancement of knowledge; every day, we hear talk of reducing investment in research.

We must resist these attacks against our universities and the enterprise of thought, for we need them more than ever. We need them for the good they do and always have done; but we need them now even more, because there are several important features of the way universities operate that make them a potential counterforce to the secular dogmatism rife in society.

First, in contrast to our political landscape, with its polarized viewpoints and disaggregated special interests, those within our universities who are engaged in research and the advancement of knowledge share the understanding that their work builds on that of others and increases knowledge for all.

Second, at least ideally, the work in the university is inherently dialogic and collegial. Critique and commentary are part of the process of validation.

Third, the progress of knowledge within our universities occurs in a transparent, testable process in which everyone can participate, wherever they live, whatever their formal title. If a mathematician in Mumbai can disprove a theory conceived in New York, no amount of misplaced elitism or nationalism can invalidate his argument. Or, if a clerk in the patent office in Bern, Switzerland, develops breakthrough theories in physics, it does not matter that there is not yet the title "professor" before his name.

Fourth and finally, the ultimate test of work done in the university is time. A scholar's reward is the durability of his or her work, potentially over generations. Inevitably, there are false starts. Some results, fashionable for a time, are rejected after further examination. Others, initially dismissed as foolish, later come to be seen as brilliant.

Beyond these important structural features inherent in a university's work, there are characteristics that are more a matter of attitude than of formal process. Chief among these is the combination of boldness and humility—boldness in conceptualizing a new thought; humility in offering it for review by others. Those who claim discovery are subject to the norms of their fields. They make their sources accessible and respond to questions according to well-honed standards, a process that is not for the timid or those who cannot brook criticism.

Some years ago, in his book *Working Without a Net*, my NYU colleague Dick Foley argued, I think correctly, that in a university there can be no final resting place for inquiry.[14] This view is the exact antipode of secular dogmatism. On our campuses, no viewpoint can be so secure that it cannot be challenged. Citizens of the university must temper their convictions with a commitment to invite challenges. There cannot be orthodoxy; no viewpoint is above reproach in the world of knowledge. Some propositions become axioms for the moment, worthy of further development—that is, until they, too, are superseded or disproved.

Our colleges and universities do not have a monopoly on such exchanges. In a well-functioning democratic society, the contest of ideas should take place in multiple venues, from pulpit to press. But as the quality of dialogue in much of our society becomes impoverished, universities become "sacred spaces" for critical reflection. By this phrase, I do not mean the kind of sacred space to which one retreats for contemplation or withdrawal from the world. In the face of the assault on thought, universities might well be tempted to seize such a defensive posture behind sheltered walls, to insulate themselves. But such a withdrawal would be irresponsible and destructive for both the university and society. Universities are, indeed, protected areas for thought and dialogue; but, precisely because they enjoy the benefit of protection and thus a special capacity to incubate ideas, they have a duty to mobilize outward from their protected position to become even greater forces than they now are for the advancement of thought and dialogue in society generally.

This culture of devalued thought requires a cure; universities must provide the antidote. They must stand as witnesses for their core values and act as a reproach to dogmatism and its consequences. They must extend their most salient internal activity—the meaningful testing of ideas—as a model for wider public discourse. Simply put, they are our best hope for reversing the ominous trends permeating our society.

There are steps we must take if our universities are to play this role. I turn to this in the next part of this book.

2

The Traditional University as Sacred Space for Discourse

Prelude

I entered high school in January 1956. Those of us who began that month had to complete freshman year by the end of August to start sophomore year in September; there was no time for any extracurricular activities. As I began my sophomore year, however, Charlie Winans, the mentor par excellence, intervened, urging that I get involved: "You must broaden yourself. Go be a debater. I think you'll be good at it." He thereby framed my view of discourse in ways I would not appreciate for decades.

Debaters have to be at ease with both thoughts and words. Even as they present their own argument, they must anticipate the strongest possible formulation of the opposing position. And they must be able to address directly that opposing argument, exposing its flaws. When their opponents respond, they have to engage the response by taking their own argument to the next level, a process top debaters call "extending" ("deepening") the argument. This iterative extension of argument is the essence of competitive debate. A debater who repeats a point without taking into account the counterargument presented by an opponent has no chance of getting the judge's ballot at the end of the round.

The structure of formal debate forces debaters on both sides to extend the argument. The first affirmative opens by stating the interpretation of the resolution he or she will defend, and then supports the resolution with an argument. The first negative responds with counterattacks. The debate then proceeds until there have been eight speeches in all, four by each side, each building upon and extending the points made in earlier stages. The arguments may be sophisticated, but the process is simple: Progressively push the discussion—or lose.

A normal tournament weekend is structured so that top debaters have to probe the topic in all its complexity. Over the two or three days of a typical tournament, debaters might engage in as many as eight debates, alternating between the affirmative and the negative; thus, a winning debater must be prepared for both sides on any variation of the topic. This aspect of debate inculcates in all participants the capacity to see both sides and the gray in between.

Another feature of the style of debate I favor most is that every tournament, week in and week out for the full academic year, focuses on a single topic—for example, "Resolved: The United States should require compulsory service for all citizens," or "Resolved: The United Nations should be significantly strengthened." This element gives added meaning to the notion of "extending" the argument: top debaters must advance their thinking on the subject as the season progresses. The very best are under mounting pressure, since many tournaments feature a public final debate between the top two teams of the week, with the other teams as the audience—teams who would be debating the week's winners a week or two later at another tournament on the same topic, having heard (in the public round) the strongest arguments employed by the winners. No team could rest on its laurels; no team was safe at the top.

My love for debate also was nurtured in the early 1960s, when, as a young but passionate advocate, I ventured forth from my cloistered Brooklyn to Union Square in Manhattan. A short subway ride took me to a different world, where people debated the issues of the day not in tournaments but in the cauldron of political activism.

In those days, Union Square was a famously informal public forum with an avid and sometimes rowdy audience, a setting that encouraged wide-ranging public arguments over politics, religion, science, and just about any other topic. In my earliest forays there, I stoutly defended an orthodox Catholic perspective that was frequently the subject of attacks from vocal atheists, agnostics, or others critical of my Church. Soon, I was engaged in debates on public policy issues. I visited the Square almost every week in the summer, sometimes for "scheduled debates" on the Friday "card" and even for the "main event," which featured adversaries who stood on the pedestal of the equestrian statue.

Looking back, I realize that even these debates were characterized by thoughtfulness and serious discourse, again with an extension of the argument. They certainly did not have the iterative depth associated with the year-long probing of an annual debate topic. Yet, they were far more than a simpleminded articulation of first-level talking points. The participants lived in a world of ideas and were committed to testing their views. Often, public discussion in the Square was followed by hours of exchanges over coffee.

So it was that my early intellectual life was framed. Competitive debate taught me that reward came from a true encounter between differing viewpoints; that critical policy issues are gray, not black and white; and, that listening carefully is important, because debaters must do their best to respond to what their opponents have actually said. Debaters succeed not by talking louder or shouting or threatening or booing or hissing, but by offering responsive arguments at every stage of the discussion.

After nearly twenty years in this environment, I was primed to embrace a grounded intellectual pluralism. Given this background, it will not come as a surprise that I believe our society, suffering as it is from the pathology of secular dogmatism, would be well served if it embraced the values and processes I found decades ago in the classrooms, auditoriums, and even squares where those debates occurred.

Universities are natural settings for nurturing these habits of mind; but our campuses are not immune from the trends that are roiling society. First, as the commitment to serious thought has diminished, universities, the stewards of thought, themselves have been devalued; ultimately, the public has been less and less willing to provide the resources to sustain research and learning. Second, as a secular dogmatism has increasingly permeated society, university communities have become infected, causing them to suffer from the very disease they might cure.

Beyond these general threats, our universities face, from outside and from within, several more specific threats to their integrity as sacred spaces for dialogue. Even as we work to safeguard our campuses against the general threats that endanger all of society, we would do well to understand these more specific threats, so that they do not amplify the impact of general threats on our campuses.

Threats from Outside the Sacred Space

Every university president, provost, and dean can tell tales of external pressure on the active dialogue they seek to cultivate, most often in the form of calls to ban an objectionable speaker or controversial material from campus.

My first such experience came early in my time as dean of the NYU law school, when a campus group invited the Cuban minister of justice, Carlos Amat, to a "dinner conversation." A congressman used a Miami radio station to mobilize a protest campaign against the event. I received hundreds of faxes every day condemning the fact that this man, viewed by many as responsible for repression in Cuba, was to appear at NYU. The faxes ignored our insistence that the minister adhere to rules that applied to all who spoke at the law school—among them, that the speaker agree to stand for questioning for twice as long as he or she spoke.

The evening was one of the most memorable events of my time as dean. We had reserved twenty-four seats—about 80 percent of those invited—for Cuban-American law students. A faculty member, who decades earlier had written the State Department's draft of the Cuban Embargo, acted as moderator. The student guests at the dinner sat silently during the meal, refusing even to touch a fork, lest they be seen as breaking bread with such a man. Then, they questioned Amat intensely, against the background chant of protesters outside the building.

The day after the event, I received a fax—not of protest, but of apology—from the congressman in Miami who had incited the campaign against the visit. The students had informed him that the event had given them an important forum, allowing them to give voice to their views.

Such apologies are rare. Far more common are letters of condemnation, from all sides of the political spectrum. One case close to my intellectual home involved Father Daniel Berrigan, the high school teacher who, in 1956, wrote the Latin words for "outside the Church there is no salvation" on the blackboard of my classroom. In those early years, we knew Father Berrigan as a charismatic teacher and talented poet; a decade later, we and the world knew him as a leader of the opposition to American involvement in Vietnam. There was no middle ground on Danny Berrigan. Some (including me) saw him as a hero, while others thought he was a traitor. Forty years on, when Fordham University installed him as its poet-in-residence, Fordham's alumni magazine was filled with letters condemning the university's administration for doing so. Dean Jeffrey von Arx, later the president of Fairfield University, responded by saying he was confident that "Fordham students have the critical abilities to judge whether they agree with his or any other opinion."[1]

There are a fair number of people who refuse to listen to a political bête noire and are committed to preventing others from doing so. Often, these would-be censors are people with power—or at least with leverage. Before I formally assumed the presidency of NYU, just months after Bill Clinton had left the White House, one of the university's most significant benefactors threatened to withdraw his gifts (at the time, over $100 million) unless I canceled a symposium, to be led by President Clinton, on the challenges of a globalized world.

This man, who would have had us deprive our students and faculty of the opportunity to engage with President Clinton, would likely have been pleased if we had chosen to welcome Richard Nixon in the days after his resignation. And I am certain that among those who gladly welcomed President Clinton, many would have excoriated us had we invited President Nixon. I would welcome both on campus, and I think that any university true to its values would as well. In the case of President Clinton, we went forward with the event, risking loss of the donor. The day was a great success. And, although no apology came from the donor (as one had from the congressman), he has continued to be one of the most generous contributors to the university.

These three examples are similar but distinct. The Cuban minister had been invited by a club. Father Berrigan was being given an honor. President Clinton had brought to NYU's law school a globally important event, broadcast around the world, which he had organized. Although each case involved the familiar scenario of external pressure to silence a speaker, each presented different questions, and, in my view, each case type ought to prompt different standards and responses. I will discuss these variations in detail later. For now, I note what the examples have in common: They each involve opposition—and a cry for censorship—from an individual or group that viewed the invited speaker as unworthy of a university platform.

As common as such instances are, they pale in comparison to the now-ubiquitous organized efforts to restrict conversations on campus touching certain topics in "objectionable" ways. "Watch groups" seek to ferret out and sanction speakers or even professors over views to which they object. Forswearing debate, these efforts are often complemented by aggressive, well-funded public campaigns that attack professors, departments, or schools for expressing "unacceptable" opinions. With no sense of irony, these campaigns sometimes fly under the flag of guaranteeing "balance."

Over the years, I have seen many such groups in action. Unless they meet resistance from those inside and outside our universities who appreciate the importance of genuine debate, they jeopardize the essence of our universities and impair their capacity to act as a counterforce against the disease of secular dogmatism.

Sometimes, external forces manage to enlist the power of government to pressure universities to deviate from what usually are carefully crafted rules on inclusion or exclusion. One such example is the notorious Solomon Amendment (named, not for the wise king, but for its sponsor, the late Representative Gerald Solomon), an attempt to use law to force universities to ignore their written policies against discrimination on the basis of race, religion, nationality, gender, or sexual orientation. Under the amendment, universities could not deny a spot at placement fairs to military recruiters, even though the recruiters refused to sign the standard pledge forswearing discrimination (specifically, in their case, forswearing discrimination based on sexual orientation). Universities that denied access to the military faced the draconian prospect of losing tens or even hundreds of millions of dollars in governmental support for programs ranging from financial aid to medical research.

Eventually the military changed its policy, nullifying the controversy over the Solomon Amendment. However, in recent times, a proposed ban on military service by transgender Americans may be reviving some discriminatory policies and creating new ones.

After the attack on September 11, 2001, the euphemistically named Patriot Act forced librarians to provide FBI agents with personal reader information, or even to hand over library computers.[2] Moreover, the act prevented libraries from protecting their borrowers against government surveillance—and it barred them from informing students, teachers, or researchers if their choice of reading was being watched and recorded. These extreme measures were very troubling.

Perhaps more understandably, for a period of time after the attacks, the government erected barriers to make it more difficult to bring foreign professors and students to American universities. Scholars faced longer application periods, extensive background checks, and constant monitoring; many were, in effect, denied entry. There were some clearly unnecessary precautions, however: For example, some of the scholars were seeking only to return, after brief visits home, to universities where they already had spent months or even years without posing a security threat. In any case, the overall result was that, in the years just after the attacks, the number of foreign scholars coming to American schools stagnated, reversing a fifty-year trend of increased enrollment,[3] depleting our capacity to understand other cultures, and diminishing the prospect that they would understand ours.

As the nation recovered from the trauma of 2001, and as we refined our screening policies, the flow of foreign scholars into our universities increased again—notably, with no impact on security.[4] In a positive step, the government created the National Security Higher Education Advisory Board, on which I served during both the Bush and Obama administrations. This board brought university presidents into a conversation with Homeland Security and agencies such as the FBI and CIA in an effort to attain the right balance between, on the one hand, security concerns and, on the other, the ability of universities to include foreign scholars in the campus conversation, which itself enhances security and national interests.

When the overbroad 2017 travel ban threatened that balance, at first the courts and then the Supreme Court restored equilibrium. But the hostility associated with the new travel policies took a toll. After a decade of tremendous growth in the number of foreign students coming to American campuses, there was a sharp drop in international enrollment around the country. In the first year of the Trump administration, the number of new foreign students declined by 7 percent.[5] It remains to be seen how extensive or enduring the effect of the modified ban, now approved by the Supreme Court, will be in coming years.

However, the travel ban, targeted as it was at Muslim countries, was not the only threat to the flow of scholars. In 2018, the White House announced plans, as part of a broad package of measures targeting China, to limit dramatically the flow of students and scholars from that country to American universities and colleges;[6] over the prior three years, over three hundred thousand such students had come.[7] Putting aside the adverse trade effects of the new policy (over $12 billion flows annually from these students into the American economy),[8] from a foreign policy and security perspective this attack on dialogue and mutual understanding is unfortunate. For example, reasonable people would say it is in our national interest that half the members of President Xi's cabinet have children being educated here.[9]

It is worrisome that, in all these initiatives, once again the power of government is being marshaled against the traditions of inclusion and dialogue that have made our universities great. The threat of terrorism surely justifies sensible security measures; and our leaders must negotiate vigorously with China over trade and other matters. However, regulations that pander to prejudices and xenophobia only undermine the long-term security of our country by closing our doors to gifted professors and students who almost always depart appreciative of our nation, its people, and its values, and who become goodwill ambassadors for the United States wherever they live.

Beyond such obvious threats to the university, there are other, subtler, pernicious forces at work, not least among them diminished public funding of research.[10] Remarkably, these cuts are being made as governments around the globe are emphasizing creativity and innovation across all fields. There is undeniable irony in America's retreat from investment not only in the arts and the social sciences but also in the hard sciences, even as others seek to create centers of research and learning modeled on the American university as a generator of progress.

In sum, the external threats to the university as sacred space are both episodic and systemic, both obvious and subtle. Powerful individuals and groups often make the threats, and they sometimes succeed in enlisting the government as an ally. Then, of course, there are public officials who disdain universities, what they do, and (in some cases) even thought itself. These threats must be taken seriously; it is fair to say that they are well known to the leaders of our universities and indeed are taken quite seriously by them.

Threats from Within the Sacred Space

Some of the most aggressive critics of our universities would minimize the importance of the external threats to our campuses, insisting instead that the real threat to flourishing discourse is what they see as a growth of "political correctness" among faculty and students, abetted by complicit or unwitting university leaders. A cottage industry thrives on propagating an image of universities as ideologically captured by left-wing faculty and administrators; but, careful examination reveals that these now familiar parodies are built on relatively isolated examples and that, simply put, they do not represent accurately the world of ideas known to those of us who live in universities. In my view, claims that our universities have been captured ideologically reflect a lack of understanding of the realities of academic life. Indeed, I believe that, more often than not, these complaints about political correctness are intended to silence voices the critics would prefer not to hear.

My view is supported by data from well-designed studies in peer-reviewed journals. Thus, a comprehensive 1984 study reported that 40 percent of professors described themselves as "liberals" or "left," 34 percent described themselves as "conservative" or "right," and 27 percent described themselves as "moderate".[11] Over two decades later, in the most recent (2007) study, 40 percent said "liberal," 9 percent said "conservative," and 46 percent (the plurality) said "moderate."[12] So, there had been no growth in the liberal contingent, which had lost its plurality position. To the extent there were fewer self-described conservatives, they had been replaced by moderates, not liberals. The same survey reported that 51 percent of respondents identified as Democrats, 14 percent identified as Republicans, and 36 percent as Independents.[13] And, importantly, similar surveys show no evidence that faculty ideology is associated with changes in the ideological orientation of students.[14]

It is also not the case that efforts to control the conversation on campus come primarily from the left. For example, a conservative organization, Turning Point USA, has circulated widely a brochure, "The Foundational Structure for Winning Back Our Universities," which is a playbook designed to help conservative students seize control of student-government and fraternity-chapter presidencies. The brochure states: "Our first and primary goal is to commandeer the top office of Student Body President at each of the most recognizable and influential American universities." It boasts that it already has "direct oversight and influence over more than $500 million in university tuition and student fee appropriations." This number is disputed, but it is noteworthy that the organization has budgeted over $2 million for such efforts over the next several years. This is not a story of "liberal capture."[15]

The key question is whether university citizens across the political spectrum feel comfortable in expressing their views in the dialogue that (we hope) characterizes our university

communities. Here, two recent studies indicate that conservative scholars say they are able to succeed and find happiness on
America's campuses. Indeed, whereas 56 percent of liberal
professors indicated they were happy with their academic careers, 66 percent of conservative professors did so.[16]

In my own experience, debate is thriving on our campuses. Indeed, it is quite common for the university leadership
to be challenged. At NYU, for example, there are regular debates
on university policy and on major issues of the day, with views
across the spectrum presented vigorously. To cite just one of
many examples, at the weekly faculty colloquium I regularly
attend at the law school, leading scholars from the left, the right,
and all points in between meet to dissect an early draft of a
colleague's work in progress; no scholar, no matter how high
his or her academic station, leaves unscathed. The School of
Athens was no better a venue for debate. I believe that in this
regard NYU and its law school are more typical than exceptional among American universities. Putting aside for the moment the special case of faith-based universities, on most
campuses most of the time no viewpoint is beyond question.

That said, the fact is that universities can do more than
they are doing to honor the commitment to openness. Even
those who are committed to the life of the mind sometimes
manifest a certitude that transforms their opinions into doctrines; and even on our campuses, conversation can become a
monologue, interrupted only occasionally by pauses to preserve
the appearance of engagement. Although the data support the
claim that there is more political diversity on our campuses
than the cottage-industry-induced conventional wisdom would
hold, the same data undeniably display a tilt to the left (especially on "elite" campuses). It would be ironic in the extreme if
the heirs to the great tradition of civil liberties were the ones

posing a threat to open inquiry and free speech on campus. Thus, we all must examine regularly our adherence to the stated principles of discourse—with the same skepticism and rigor we apply to the arguments of our critics.

It is true that on many campuses a great majority of faculty and students share a prevailing viewpoint on a wide range of issues. Indeed, the presence of such shared values—whether political, religious, academic, or social—is often the reason why faculty or students join a particular campus community. There is absolutely nothing wrong with such a common ethos: From NYU (a secular research university) to Notre Dame (a Catholic research university), from Oberlin (a secular liberal arts college) to Muhlenberg College (an evangelical Lutheran liberal arts college), universities and colleges proudly nurture identifying characteristics. The question is, however, whether the campus cultivates debate over even those views that are so widely held within a community as to be close to consensus positions.

As they work to enhance this culture of debate, university leaders must take care, lest a climate develop on campus that imposes too high a cost of participation on those whose views challenge the prevailing orthodoxy. The concern ought to be mapped, not along traditional left/right political lines, for the various political viewpoints are reasonably well represented within our universities; rather, particular effort must be devoted to welcoming those whose voices have not been heard.

Campuses, like society, may have appeared remarkably quiescent in the 1950s and early 1960s; but, we now know that this surface placidity masked a reality of exclusion. Today, we see that we as a society were ignoring voices that deserved to be heard and depriving ourselves of the insights they could have given us. Where voices of some are silenced (or ignored), or where a platform to speak is denied to some, the contest of ideas may be more comfortable, but it is less productive.

A maxim of competitive debate is relevant here: If we are to engage, we must hear; and if we are to hear, we must become better listeners. In his book *Civility,* Yale's Stephen Carter urges that in true discourse even fanatics must be met with love—with searching questions and with a listening spirit.[17] I agree.

Listening is among the deepest manifestations of respect. Yet, in society and on university campuses, little attention has been given to the art of listening, least of all listening to those with experiences and viewpoints different from one's own. My NYU colleague Carol Gilligan speaks of "radical listening," the kind that starts with a true desire to learn from the experience of others and to discover what they know. It is this kind of listening that leaders of universities must cultivate more intentionally.

Once we are prepared to listen, we must create the conversational space in which those who have not had a voice feel free to speak. Such a space can exist only in an atmosphere characterized by trust—specifically, trust in the good faith of conversational partners and their willingness to hear. Given our society's clear history of silencing certain speakers, it is unreasonable to expect all potential speakers to presume the good faith of those who traditionally have dominated the forum. The speaker who rises to articulate a position against the tide of the day or to reveal a previously closely held belief is vulnerable. If we are to create a truly dialogic space on our campuses, we must take care to ensure that the willingness to be vulnerable is rewarded.

The good news is that on campuses around the country, colleagues, students, and friends (including women, persons of color, and other marginalized communities) are beginning to find it possible to reveal their vulnerability. Those of us who have had no trouble being heard need to understand that those who express hurt as a cri de coeur are making an act of faith in us; they are, in effect, weaponizing those of us who hear their cry by listing their vulnerabilities, thereby instructing us how to be hurtful. In genuine dialogue, that act of faith must be reciprocated openly, not defensively. We listeners must make clear to those who speak that they are in a safe space for such dialogue. And all of us must turn the lens of understanding until the speaker's view becomes clear—even if it is unflattering. In the words of the poet Robert Burns: "If we could only see ourselves as others see us."[18]

As trust builds, those who are vulnerable increasingly should be able to accept the good will of those who traditionally have enjoyed less vulnerability; but, it is unreasonable to expect such acceptance in the first stage. There is too much history to overcome. Thus, in the beginning of the process and for a good while thereafter, those of us who traditionally have enjoyed voice and power must accept that we may not be viewed or heard by others as we would prefer to be; we must accept that, notwithstanding what we might feel about our own good intentions, we are not understood by all to be good. The burden of creating a truly inclusive sacred space falls on those of us who have been privileged to inhabit it over time.

Here, a specific story may be helpful.

When in 2015 campuses around the country were being roiled by debate and protests over the status and treatment of racial minorities in American society and at universities, we at NYU quickly came to a consensus that we had not lived up to our ideals of inclusivity and mutual respect. We had reached an important moment for us to take stock and to identify the work still to be done. To that end, we sought to convene our community in a forum where those who had suffered could speak openly, where the university's leadership could listen carefully, and where participants could have faith in one another and in the process.

The initial university-wide forum drew over a thousand people to the auditorium and thousands of others around the world on closed-circuit TV. I began by saying:

> All in our community come within our ambit of care. And we do care about them, because that is what a community is. Some of them attribute ill will to us; we view ourselves as virtuous. Whether we understand why they would attribute ill will to us is irrelevant. They do. And we must find out why they do and, if possible, modify our behavior so that they can have trust in us. They are telling us that they are in pain. Our first task must be to understand how we may have contributed to that pain and how we might lessen it.
>
> This place will be better if we can understand why these good people are not perceiving what we believe to be true about it and us. It may well be that they are misjudging, completely or partially. However, if they are correct at least in part, we should focus on the part of their critique that is correct and do what we can to become better. And if what they see in us is in fact how we have been, we must work hard to change. We must put defensive thoughts aside at least for today and concentrate on how we might grow.[19]

The forum received positive reviews for what it was meant to be: a beginning (but only a beginning) of a real dialogue on campus. An important part of this opening effort was that university leaders and those who traditionally enjoyed the power to speak remained silent; we listened as those who had not been heard, or who had not been sufficiently heeded, spoke. And then, the university took steps to ensure that a conversation continued in which all could speak and be heard. That conversation continues to this day.

Let me now turn briefly to a related issue.

I have argued that careful listening is critical to dialogue and understanding. So, too, is careful articulation of one's thoughts. When the proposition is stated this way, it appears tautological: Of course a serious intellectual must state his or her positions precisely, using the power of a full vocabulary to choose the words that convey exactly the thought; and, of course, such a person would choose his or her words so as to convey the thought to the audience he or she seeks to engage, with careful consideration of that audience's capacity to hear the words as they are meant to be heard.

This process is an essential part of the life of a teacher, and is instinctive for many on our campuses. Those who care about teaching adapt their methods and words to the particular set of students in front of them; such teachers understand that their words have multiple potential meanings and that there can be consequences to ignoring how they may be heard. Caring teachers adapt.

These propositions, axiomatic for seasoned advocates and effective caring teachers, should be kept in mind as I turn briefly to a subject often used by those who attack our universities as an example of political correctness run amok: the attempt by some professors, often at a student's request, to avoid microaggressions (offenses to the sensibilities of some students) in presenting material. The argument offered by critics is that acceding to the request (for example, by providing a warning that some potentially traumatizing material is forthcoming) constitutes pampering—and closes the forum to a range of ideas.

This contention is largely a red herring, dispatched easily with a reference to the core principle of communication and teaching just described. Effective speakers and teachers always attend (say "are always sensitive" if you wish) to the possibility of an unintended meaning (call it "aggression" if you want) in their speech, or to the possibility that their words might somehow distance them from their audience; they are aware that their failing to be attentive to such matters likely will diminish the effect of their message. So, they avoid the possibly offending presentation. The burden is on the speaker to communicate to the listener, not on the listener to discern the meaning of the words only as the speaker intended them.

Sometimes the issue is not merely one of wording. For example, victims of rape, or incest, or hate crimes might find it difficult to revisit the topic of their trauma without warning. There are contexts in the world beyond our campus walls where there will be no protection; but, that does not justify a professor's failing to provide protection when it can be given at little or no cost. Certainly, material that belongs in a course (a discussion of rape in a criminal law class, to cite one example) should not be eliminated. But, if a course (say, criminal law) is required, there is no harm in alerting students when potentially traumatizing material will be discussed and in excusing the absence of students who may wish to avoid the potential trigger. Students miss class for a host of far less understandable reasons, and neither the professor nor other students suffer.

I know of no case in which a professor has been required to give warnings as a condition of being in the classroom. For nearly sixty years, my own practice has been to foreshadow the next class, inherently providing such warnings well before they had a name, pejorative or laudatory. In any case, I fail to see the growing tendency to provide such warnings as a threat to robust debate; yet, I do see how it could enhance the effectiveness of the conversation on our campuses by building confidence in participants that speakers care about them.

I have discussed how we must work, within the university, to ensure that the forum for debate is sufficiently *open*. Let me now add a postscript on how we must work to prevent the forum from being *closed* by those who would silence debate.

As in society generally, there are times when a campus forum, designed for thoughtful discussion, can be seized, literally, by those who are uninterested in dialogue. The university, in its openness, is a soft target; true discussion carries the possibility that committed, persistent groups, even small minorities, may be able to dominate the conversation. The irony is obvious: The very principle that creates the debate bestows an ability to silence discussion. Volume replaces reason. The heckler is granted a veto.

It is worth noting that there is an important distinction between the hallowed right of free speech and expression in the public forum and the equally hallowed right to academic freedom within the university: Whereas in the public forum we are generally free to say what we wish with few conditions, within the university we are expected to express our views within a context of dialogue. Whatever its propriety elsewhere, the heckler's veto, used to silence debate, is inappropriate within the academy.

Those who seek to use disruption to silence speakers sometimes argue, as students at the University of Oregon did when they disrupted a speech by the university's president, that they are engaged in "an act of free speech, not a violation of it." As a matter of constitutional law, the restrictions of the Bill of Rights apply only to government actors. However, even the government sometimes may use its powers to silence some in the interest of the speech of others: Think of the government's obligation to prevent disrupters from interfering with civil rights demonstrations, for example. Whatever the constitutional law, as a matter of campus law, the rules of civility may be enforced.

To safeguard the expressive rights of all involved, there must be clear rules, articulated in advance, defining the rights and reciprocal obligations of participants in the university's forums—open, limited, or closed. These rules must be widely disseminated throughout the university community and combined with meaningful and enforceable penalties for violators (usually best administered with a dose of patience). In my experience, such an approach goes a long way toward maintaining a productive exchange of ideas.

Before leaving this topic, I must note one other, quite subtle, potential impediment to the contest of ideas: a contortion of a strength of the academic enterprise—rigorous disciplinary norms—into a threat to it. Generations of scholars have developed the defining norms of each discipline. Such norms are guideposts, essential to preserving the advancement of thought over time. But leaders of universities must take care that a methodological orthodoxy does not develop within disciplinary units so dominant that it cannot be questioned. For example, it would be problematic if a political science department were so committed to rational choice theory that it could not find a place for a public intellectual who had run several presidential campaigns. Or if an economics department were so tied to Keynesian economics that no other theory could be taught. In many cases, a singular theoretical commitment of this sort within a discipline might simply be a strategic choice to pursue excellence in a focused way. Even so, departments making such a strategic choice should work to encourage debate about alternative approaches—for example by funding visitors from other institutions with different views. There should never be one true faith in an academic discipline.

The University Leader as Guardian of Sacred Space

There are those—and I am one—who have embraced life in the university precisely because it is a place for the contest of ideas and critical thinking. Those outside the university who express concern about the dominance of political correctness or the suppression of speech on campus should know that legions inside the university are deeply passionate about free expression. As internal champions of often clashing ideas, we fight to ensure that our campuses are safe places for the exchange of ideas, however controversial. And, by and large, we are succeeding. To cite just one indicator: the "disinvitation database" of the Foundation for Individual Rights in Education records only thirty-five attempts to disinvite guests in 2017, down from forty-five the year before—and this in a country that has over four thousand colleges and universities that bring tens of thousands of guests to campus every year.[20]

An NYU colleague, Jonathan Haidt, notes that those forces that do attempt to silence speakers come from both the left and the right. In response, he has spearheaded the Heterodox Academy, a nationwide association of professors and graduate students who seek "to improve the quality of research and education in universities by increasing viewpoint diversity, mutual understanding, and constructive disagreement."[21] Members of the Heterodox Academy have endorsed this bracing statement: "I believe that university life requires that people with diverse viewpoints and perspectives encounter each other in an environment where they feel free to speak up and challenge each other. I am concerned that many academic fields and universities currently lack sufficient viewpoint diversity—particularly political diversity. I will support viewpoint diversity in my academic field, my university, my department, and my classroom."[22] Not surprisingly, Jonathan's efforts have been met with great enthusiasm on university campuses. This spontaneous statement of principle is both evidence that the fragile sacred space needs steadfast defenders and powerful testimony that champions have risen to the cause.

In a 2018 survey of universities and college presidents, 98 percent rated promoting inclusion and (separately) protecting free speech as either very important or extremely important; 96 percent, if forced to choose, would prefer allowing students to be exposed to many types of speech rather than protecting them by prohibiting speech.[23] This is notable because chief among the noble cohorts protecting dialogue must be those specifically charged with guarding the university: the president, the provost, and the deans. For simplicity, in what follows I refer only to the president (the university position I most recently have held); however, the points made are generally applicable to those in any of the three positions.

As a threshold issue, each university president must decide whether to use his or her position to express views on a broad range of public questions, drawing on the university's capital to advance causes he or she believes are just. Harvard's legendary Charles Eliot invented the notion of the presidential bully pulpit. During his forty-year tenure as Harvard's leader and for eighteen years thereafter, he spoke on every issue of the day: from religion to foreign policy, to immigration, to antitrust, and, of course, to higher education. He was often referred to as "America's Foremost Citizen," and there is no doubt that the title accurately described his role among elites.[24]

Many observers have decried the absence of latter-day Charles Eliots, citing what they see as the relative timidity of university presidents today. True, our university leaders have been less prone to making public pronouncements—and not because of a lack of encouragement. In my years as NYU's president, I was urged to take a stand on everything from the morality of the invasion of Iraq to whether the Yankees should have allowed Alex Rodriguez to return to the team after his suspension for using steroids. The first question I was asked as NYU's president was whether there should be a separate dog run in Washington Square Park for small dogs.

I am no apologist for silence chosen for the wrong reasons; no jury would convict me of being a timid man. But during my tenure as NYU's president I consciously chose not to walk Eliot's path. And I made the choice as a matter of deep and sometimes difficult-to-maintain principle, arising from my belief that the paramount duty of the president is to safeguard the sacred space of the university for dialogue. To this end, I decided that it was essential, in order to maintain the credibility of my commitment as guardian of NYU's dialogic space, that I refrain from expressing views publicly on any issue unrelated to the central mission of the institution. This rule was absolute. To make any exception by speaking out about an issue simply because I held strong beliefs about it would create an apparent, if unintended, hierarchy of policy priorities. Once I expressed a "strongly held" view, other issues on which I offered no statement would be perceived as less important to me—an example of what logicians call a "negative pregnant." To avoid this consequence, I lived by a rule of near total forbearance.

When I was dean of NYU's law school, my resolve was tested by invitations to join the public debate on matters such as the death penalty and freedom of choice on reproductive decisions, two of many legal questions on which privately I have strongly held convictions. Over the years, sometimes against intense pressure and notwithstanding my love for a good debate, I stayed the course.

In 1997, when New York City Mayor Rudy Giuliani dramatically cut the budget for Legal Aid, I was asked by a longtime friend and generous benefactor of the law school (among whose gifts was a professorship to be named for me) to join the deans of New York City's eleven other law schools in signing an open letter of protest. In pressing me, he noted that I was the only one of the twelve who had not signed. I declined, not because I disagreed that the cuts were ill-advised (they were), but because I thought something even more vital was at stake—the value of my being able to state, each time I was asked to take a position outside the purview of my immediate institutional responsibilities, that I could not do so without violating my policy of restraint, thereby compromising my ability to protect the capacity for dialogue on campus.

There is a reasonable argument to be made that in accepting the leadership of a university a leader does not forfeit the entitlement to speak freely on issues of the day—that the roles of university leader and citizen of a free society are distinct. But while this argument seems persuasive in the abstract, I think it is problematic in practice. The two roles are linked in the public mind. Frankly, far fewer people are interested in the opinions of "John from Brooklyn" than in the views of a dean or president of NYU. And, labeling the views as "personal" does not change anything.

Not that university leaders need to be silent on all issues. There are times when they have a duty to speak. For example, a president has a cardinal duty to explain what makes the university's commitment to discourse so valuable. He or she must be resolute in resisting attacks upon the university, defending the right to offer controversial opinions, and opposing any attempt to impose political litmus tests, whether from the right or the left.

In fulfilling this duty, a president must make clear that to participate in the forum is a privilege, with attendant responsibilities. All participants must honor the commitment to debate, reflection, and respect for others. This dialogic ideal is hard to realize, but if a university president does not insist upon these responsibilities as part of the contract among members of the community, he or she will become an accomplice in subverting the sacred space.

On other occasions, a university leader has an obligation to speak. Some clear instances involve such questions as the position of universities in liberal democracies, access to education, the impact of various government decisions on higher education, and the contours of financial aid and admissions policies. On such matters, the president should enter the public arena to advance vigorously a view of what is best for the university and for society. University presidents are, after all, leaders of institutions with important roles in our culture, and they should freely express their thoughts about protecting or advancing those roles. Indeed, it would be quite impossible for the president of a university to refrain from taking positions on issues of this kind, because the operation of the university day to day depends on how they are resolved.

Even those who accept the principle of restraint I have articulated may differ on whether a particular matter falls within the category of subjects about which a university leader should speak. Some will define what is "central" to the university more broadly than I do; others more narrowly. National financial aid policy and the need for affirmative action in admissions are, for me, easily within the core. The importance of science as the basis for policy and the importance of fact as opposed to opinion in debate also make the cut. But the wisdom of a particular military intervention or various approaches to protecting the environment would not, at least for me, be "central" as I am using the term here.

Many I respect, some of whom accept my forbearance approach in principle, might disagree with me on whether a particular instance is in or out of the core. As president of Berkeley, my friend Bob Berdahl wrote a 2003 column in the *San Francisco Chronicle* opposing the Bush foreign policy;[25] later, in the *Berkeley Alumni Magazine*, he explained that he did so because he believed that the changes in notions of constitutional governance that led to that policy would play out in ways detrimental to Berkeley's future.[26] I disagree with Bob's argument, but I cannot say with certainty that he is wrong. We both agree that a general policy of restraint is wise.

In the end the vulnerability of the sacred space for dialogue justifies the conviction that those of us entrusted with the responsibility of protecting it cannot deviate from that core mission. It is more important than ever that university leaders be perceived first and foremost as facilitators of the open, public scrutiny of ideas. When the protector of debate takes a stand on issues unrelated to the higher education portfolio, he or she risks alienating those on campus who may hold a different view. Inevitably, if partiality is displayed in one case, participants in the forum will come to ask whether in other cases claims of impartiality are credible. The ability of the president to protect the sacred space turns on his or her moral authority. And that moral authority depends on a perception of fairness, which is more likely to exist if the president observes the practice of restraint I have described.

Whatever view of the president's right and duty to speak is adopted, he or she will have to make decisions—some easy, others quite difficult. Some of the tougher cases involve a decision about whether a particularly controversial external speaker should be allowed to use the university as a forum to offer his or her views. As I noted earlier, the application of principles can vary with the context: An invitation issued by the president to speak at commencement, for example, bestows a measure of dignity and stature on the speaker; on the other hand, many platforms within the university (participation in a debate, for example) do not bestow any ratification. In such cases, there should be a presumption in favor of providing a platform.

Every university should have standing rules for all external speakers who come to campus. Such rules might include the role of the moderator, the order of speakers, interruptions, and a queue for those with questions or comments. And, there should be rules of a more substantive nature, such as a requirement that speakers engage concepts, not attack persons; that those who disagree be given time to voice their disagreement; that rules of confidentiality be honored. Finally, the university may insist upon appropriate security for events on campus or elsewhere under its aegis.

However, whatever the rules, no external speaker has an absolute right to speak on campus. Each September, for example, as heads of state assemble in New York for the opening of the United Nations General Assembly, the city's universities receive dozens of requests for a platform on campus for a "major" speech by the national leader. Since it is impossible to accommodate all the requests, the president's office inevitably curates whether or not space will be made available—and under what conditions.

The issue here is not a question of censorship but of selection. No speaker has been invited; therefore, none can be disinvited. The president's role is to ask whether granting space to the proposed speaker enhances the conversation on campus.

In 2007, when Mahmoud Ahmadinejad, then president of Iran, requested a podium to speak at NYU, we denied his request; Columbia allowed him to speak. Columbia's president, Lee Bollinger, preceded Ahmadinejad's talk with a challenge to the speaker that he address certain questions; he also insisted that Ahmadinejad answer questions from the audience. In my view, either response is defensible, since the decision to include or exclude the speaker was simply an exercise of curatorial discretion.

A different case is presented when a unit of the university (a student club, a faculty seminar, a program, a department, or an institute) already has invited a speaker to campus. Here, the presumption in favor of allowing the speaker's voice to be heard is very strong—within the articulated rules for all who come to speak.

So, for example, if an authorized student club were to announce a panel to discuss the Arab-Israeli conflict, including a speaker who regularly argued that Palestinian Arabs have been so victimized that even the attacks of September 11 can be explained, I believe that the panel should be allowed to proceed, subject only to the rules of engagement and whatever additional security is required in the judgment of campus security professionals. The distinction is that inclusion avoids censorship within the sacred space without implying any university endorsement, whereas in a case where the university itself offers an invitation (Ahmadinejad) an imprimatur might be inferred.

I accept that there will be short-term costs—perhaps considerable—to the appearance of a controversial speaker.

There will be those who will be hurt or profoundly alienated, and those who will withdraw support from the university, at least for a time. There will be some with considerable power who will marshal forces in government or other key sectors to sanction or penalize the university or its leader. And there will be the tumult of protests or other actions on campus. Moreover, there sometimes will be significant direct costs: In one recent case, a Florida university spent $600,000 to provide security for an event featuring a controversial speaker—an amount equaling the in-state tuition of a thousand students.[27]

Nonetheless, the short-term costs will be dwarfed by the long-term gains resulting from honoring the presumption of inclusion. Indeed, the long-term costs of exclusion, which in this case would involve a president's restricting the right of members of the university community to shape their conversation within the bounds of civil discourse, would be staggering. Paradoxically, since there often is no way to avoid significant short-term costs whatever one does, it only makes sense to take the long-term view. Thus, though the temptation to retreat into a more comfortable conversational space is alluring, it is quite antithetical to the nature of the university—and must be resisted.

There are thoughtful observers—including some of the best thinkers on the Constitution's First Amendment—who argue that the only appropriate limits on speech are restrictions of time and place, never of substance. This position initially was very attractive to me. If imported as a governing rule to guide universities, the university would be open to all who are invited with no exceptions, and no position would be barred, however inconsistent with conventional thought, however repugnant to some, however hurtful the message.

As an absolute rule, this approach has the virtue of making decisions easier. I abandoned it only after extensive discussion with colleagues. I now believe that there are rare cases when a policy of absolute access is neither defensible nor prudent, even where an invitation has been issued by a unit or club. A clear example is a speaker who offers direct incitement to violence. Such cases of exclusion must be the proverbial exceptions that prove the rule; and, a clear explanation justifying the exception must be provided.

Given the reality that universities should and will host controversial speakers, an additional point deserves mention. The university will be better able to sustain its position as a dialogic space if controversial speakers are a part of a menu of speakers (perhaps over a period of time) in which others, with contrary viewpoints, are featured. The space for dialogue is shrinking because we have allowed critics to exploit one-off, high-visibility events featuring speakers with provocative messages. Social media empowers these critics to foment discord by caricaturing what is actually happening on campus. By presenting speakers from across a spectrum of ideas, universities help dilute the impact of any single appearance, which will help to contextualize the extreme cases and reduce the inevitable reaction.

In my view, it is clear that the role of the university leader as guardian of the sacred space is essential to creating the kind of dialogic space we seek. In the day-to-day life of a university, there are judgment calls to be made; it falls to the president, fallible as he or she may be, to exercise that authority. I have tried here to sketch several principles to guide those who are willing to play this role:

First, when the university's imprimatur might be implied, as with an honorary degree or named lecture, the president may exercise judicious restraint. There is nothing inappropriate about such restraint, so long as it does not chill the willingness to be provocative.

Second, when an authorized unit of the university invites a speaker, no matter how controversial, it is usually inappropriate for the university's leadership to ban that speaker.

Third, the university's leadership must accept an affirmative obligation actively to expand the appetite of people for the unheard voice and the unconsidered insight. This obligation is best met by developing frameworks and structures that contextualize the various opinions and provide the balance that enriches the conversation. Platitudes on the importance of discourse in one-off situations will not suffice.

And fourth, in making judgments about access to the university's forum, its leadership must adhere to the principles of scholarly conversation and display the qualities of dispassion, thoroughness, and resistance to sensationalism that characterize the best evidence-based thinking within the university.

The Dialogic Compact among University Citizens

There is an important distinction between external actors, whose participation in the university dialogue is transient and, therefore, discretionary, and internal actors who are more permanent members of the community. Both external and internal speakers, by accepting participation, enter a compact, but the compacts are different. I already have listed the conditions and rules that might apply to external actors who enter the dialogic space. These rules also are applicable to internal actors, but internal actors both enjoy additional rights and assume additional obligations.

Academic freedom protects free inquiry and expression by internal actors, although this cherished right must never be taken for granted and must be guarded zealously. All within the university must be free from censorship and censure. The assurance that each member of the community can explore unpopular ideas without threat of reprisal secures the university's mission. This protection is essential and applies to students, teaching assistants, adjuncts, and professors. Academic freedom is more fundamental than tenure, because it must apply to all.

But a discussion of the relationship between academic freedom and the sacred dialogic space of the university is incomplete if it focuses only on the protection that academic freedom offers to the individual; it must connect the rights such freedom confers with the responsibility to protect the forum. For internal actors, the acceptance of membership in the university community implies a reciprocal fealty to the principle that governs that forum—the inviolability of open debate and engagement, especially among those who hold opposing views. We must never forget that the unfamiliar, which might seem to some bizarre or even idiotic, is precisely what must be protected. In a university, no thought is above reproach.

Early in the process of attracting and admitting students, a university should make clear it is an axiom of the enterprise that orthodoxies will be challenged. And that must be exemplified in the daily life of the institution. For a university to become an exemplar of a dialogic community, it must raise the consciousness of every actor in the system and create an ethos of dialogue among all who comprise the university: from the most august faculty member to the resident student assistants in the dorms. *Res ipsa loquitur:* "The thing speaks for itself."

There are many ways to embrace difference. One is to shape an internal population that brings to the table a truly diverse set of experiences and viewpoints. But embracing diversity in this way requires creating space (the sacred space) where everyone in the community simultaneously feels able to move out of his or her comfort zone in honest dialogue and feels safe in doing so.

Every participant has vulnerabilities, but students are more vulnerable to the discomforts of difficult conversation than those (such as faculty) who are more experienced in discourse. A goal of the university, as it initiates students into the contest of ideas, should be to help them become comfortable with their vulnerability. This is not an easy task: If teachers, mentors, and peers are overprotective, they risk paternalism; if underprotective, they risk undermining the students' capacity to enter this new territory. Worse yet, they risk causing real pain—pain that might make students recoil from subsequent dialogue.

One effective way to imprint in the intellectual and social DNA of young people the habit of engagement is to make debate central to the undergraduate experience. Through debate, students can explore complex issues under formal rules. They can learn how to formulate and defend their positions on those issues—and then how to bring their views to the public square.

It is our responsibility to create a culture on campus that celebrates conversation in every form. We should cultivate a community that will motivate all our students to learn the skills of presenting a position, listening to others' positions, and deepening the exchange with considered, fact-based argument to reach a reasoned consensus, or at least to educate opposing sides to find new clarity about their differences. Faculty and peers committed to this ideal can motivate students to be informed and to be active participants in the contest of ideas on campus.

An Uncommon Case: When the Guardian Does Speak

I noted that a president should observe a rule of "*nearly* total forbearance" from expressing political views on issues unrelated to the university's core activities. This articulation implied that there are rare circumstances when the president should address issues beyond those affecting the mission and practices of the university and the guardianship of the space for dialogue. One such example was the apartheid debate on campuses in the late 1970s and early 1980s. On that question, a virtually unanimous consensus developed throughout our country that justified public statements and related actions.

It is vital, however, that even these instances be circumscribed, in recognition of the fact that it is impossible for the president to speak out without drawing down the moral capital of the university. Moreover, even on matters like apartheid, a president should not speak out on his or her own authority; rather, he or she should assume the bully pulpit only after following procedures designed to demonstrate consensus within the university community—and only after consensus has been attained.

Similarly, attempts to use the university's endowment as an instrument for political expression are usually misguided. Conversations over the years at NYU with those who wanted to use our endowment in this way reinforced this point for me. At various times advocates urged divestment from interests as diverse as defense contractors, the fossil fuel industry, companies that run private prisons, or those with interests in particular countries. Some said we should not use Citibank for student loans; others argued that we should not invest in government bonds.

The best approach is to create a venue for dialogue that might elicit a consensus in the university community on a particular issue. Although reaching consensus will be rare, every university should have a process for doing so lodged in its representative bodies. The ultimate decision on whether a consensus exists should reside in the governing board of the university (usually the board of trustees). And everyone within the university should understand from the outset that there will be very few cases that will warrant the university investing its political capital this way, because that capital must be husbanded for the university's research and learning role.

The process leading to these exceptions should involve formal procedures. And it should be clear that a simple majority of those at the university (faculty, students, administrators, and others) is not enough to justify action. Rather, there must be overwhelming support within the university community for the proposed position. And in some cases, even when a substantial majority favors a position, the president or the governing board may conclude that the gravity of the arguments against it is sufficiently strong that a deviation from the default policy of restraint is ill-advised.

At NYU, the University Senate is the appropriate venue to hear arguments and to explore whether there is a consensus around the social or political use of the university's political capital or endowment. Through various councils—such as the Faculty Council, the Student Council, and the Administrative Management Council—the constituent elements of the university can express views in those cases where advocates urge university political action. If a consensus develops that the University Senate endorses, it can transmit that view to the university's administration and Board of Trustees. One notable advantage of this approach is that in the rare cases where the governing board approves political action through such a process, its endorsement has greater force and legitimacy by virtue of the formal authorization of the community than if the decisions were left to the president's discretion.

During my time as president, this process guided our campus community through a conversation begun by faculty and students eager to have the University use its endowment investment policy in support of a "green agenda." It is a source of pride at NYU that, well before the issue of using our endowment to make a political statement on environmental policy arose, the university community, through voluntary internal action, had shown leadership in adopting several environment-friendly measures. NYU was the first university to join then Mayor Michael Bloomberg's 2012 initiative to reduce the carbon footprint of major institutions in the city by 30 percent before 2016. Indeed, NYU reached the goal several years before the deadline, going beyond it to reduce its carbon footprint by nearly 50 percent. Not surprisingly, these efforts did not satisfy the most dedicated environmental activists in the NYU community. Beginning in 2014, a group of students, supported by many faculty members, urged that the university divest from any investment holdings in the fossil fuel industry.

This request could not be addressed as straightforwardly as one might imagine, since NYU's endowment holds no direct investments in any industry, but only shares in various funds—funds that typically move in and out of holdings very quickly and do not report to investors the nature of their holdings. For this reason, the disinvestment group proposed as an alternative that the university limit its investments to so-called "clean" funds (those that invest only in companies committed to a "green" agenda), an option that could be implemented more easily.

We coached the students and their allies on how to move their proposal through the university's processes to determine whether there was the requisite overwhelming consensus in the community for the university to consider action along the lines they proposed. In the end, the University Senate recommended to the governing board that the university avoid making any direct investments in fossil fuel stocks (since NYU had no such investments, this was prospective); but the Senate did not go so far as to endorse investment only in "green funds." Since the advocates knew I was personally quite attracted to their political position, they urged me to use my final days as president to announce support of their position—ignoring all the principles I had articulated and grossly underappreciating my commitment to those principles, even in cases when my private conviction was clear. My unwillingness to act distressed the students.

In concluding my consideration of this set of issues, I must address one more circumstance in which a president, as guardian of the university dialogic space, may be called upon not to speak but to act. Although cases of this sort are rare, when they arise they are significant tests of the president's moral authority and judgment. These are the cases where important viewpoints clearly are absent from a major campus conversation. In such cases, occasionally the president should intervene to preserve a balance.

I have argued that university leaders should not promote personal political or social views, and that to do so would devalue their voices when they are most needed—when there is an evident danger to dialogue, when there is a need to advocate for the research and learning enterprise itself, or when the community as a whole has urged the president to speak publicly on a controversial issue.

But, when he or she encounters circumstances when a voice is unrepresented in campus discourse, he or she should consider using the authority to invite speakers to add the needed viewpoint to the discussion. Such intervention in the conversation could occur in different ways—most often by identifying speakers whose viewpoints, although widely respected, are absent on campus. It is important, however, that such intervention be relatively rare and clearly justified, lest the corrective action be construed as an endorsement of a particular position.

On the same logic, though in a different domain, the president might encourage the admissions team to consider favorably an applicant's potential contribution to dialogue on campus. There is evidence of such attention among campus leaders to diversity of viewpoint. An Inside Higher Ed survey of university leaders in the fall of 2017 found that 38 percent of schools were intensifying their efforts to recruit from rural areas, 30 percent were putting increased efforts into recruiting from poor white areas, and 8 percent were working harder to find conservative students.[28]

There are practical limits to the president's role as the protector of balance on campus. It is plainly impossible to make sure that all sides of all issues are being heard at all times in all university venues. A corrective action that addresses one issue where reputable viewpoints are missing inevitably will leave other imbalances in place. In this, as in other areas, the perfect should not be the enemy of the good.

The Sacred Space and People of Faith

One test of whether authentic dialogue is taking place at a university is whether people of faith can be in conversation with others. This is so because people of faith often have a distinct source for some of their knowledge: revelation. Revelation is not the product of critical reasoning, but it is a significant component of a life of faith. Important as it may be to the believer, however, revelation cannot count as argument in the contest of ideas; it has a very different provenance. How, then, might people of faith participate in the contest? How can the university as "sacred space" welcome the religious?

All who participate in the dialogue on campus must embrace a desire to think through the other person's viewpoint and understand the terms of his or her perspective. Under this rubric, although dogmatism is not welcome within the university, religious people are. But this welcome is extended on terms consistent with the university's essence. People of faith are not barred from participation simply because some of their beliefs arise from sources that cannot be tested in debate. That said, they must accept that their revelation and the consequent "truths" based upon faith cannot be offered as argument.

I have lived on both sides of the division between faith and reason. For years, I struggled with how, where, and even whether to discuss my faith. I was concerned that doing so might be inconsistent with my role as the president of a secular university.

Not long after the election of Pope Benedict XVI in 2005, I was invited to deliver the commencement address at Fordham University, the university from which I received a PhD in religion. I felt called upon to use the occasion to explore my concerns about what I viewed as Benedict's retrogressive and quite repressive theological dogmatism, antithetical to the Vatican Council's ecumenical spirit. I went so far as to write a draft of an address suggesting that the graduates join with others in the "body" of the Church writ large to instruct the pope on such matters as in vitro fertilization and the importance of contraception in Africa's struggle against AIDS.

But I never delivered that speech—in no small part because my wife, Lisa, reminded me how carefully I had refrained from making statements on any matter not directly related to my work on behalf of NYU. As she put it in her closing argument: "NYU has no stake in how the pope runs your Church."

At the time I was teaching a course I still teach called Baseball as a Road to God. Although the course did offer explorations of my own encounters with faith, spirituality, and the ineffable, I did not view it as a public expression of those views. When I was persuaded to develop a book on the subject, however, I had to confront the fact that my faith would be put in the public square. I was worried about the propriety of the president of a secular university expressing explicitly religious views. In retrospect, I think I allowed myself that indulgence in large part to help me process Lisa's sudden, premature death. But it also was important that two friends and colleagues with impeccable secularist credentials, Ronald Dworkin and Thomas Nagel, urged me to go forward.

When *Baseball as a Road to God* was released, Bill Moyers, who had worked often with Lisa, insisted that I appear on his PBS program, *Bill Moyers Journal*. In preparation, Bill told me that he felt he had to honor Lisa by asking how I was coping with her death and what my belief in God meant in the context of my grief.

When, as the cameras rolled, he asked, my response was straightforward: "I know Lisa still exists both as an influence on my life and the life of those she encountered, including, of course, our children. I also know that I have reflected every day on whether I am living my life in a way that is worthy of her love." Taken alone, these words were and are unremarkable. But I added other thoughts: "Through my faith, I also believe ("know") that she exists as a conscious being and that she is aware of my continuing love for her; and I believe that when I pass from this plane, she and I will be aware of our continuing love." I emphasized that I understood that my views, grounded in faith as they were, could not be offered as proof in a debate. I concluded: "Some truths cannot be discovered through debate; some truths are ineffable."

Although I was expressing a position familiar to those who knew me well, I did so with a degree of trepidation, a fear that

I was moving beyond what was appropriate for NYU's president. But when the Moyers broadcast aired, the response to my expression of faith was different from what I had anticipated. Most of the hundreds of messages from viewers said how "refreshing" it was to hear the head of a secular university speak freely about religiosity and spirituality. For me, there is no intrinsic contradiction between the dimensions of reason and faith, and I was gratified to learn that there were many who thought my role could encompass both without compromising either.

One obstacle to welcoming people of faith either within the university or in the public square is that many in universities and among the intellectual elite see themselves as inherently at odds with people of faith. Professor William Stuntz, an evangelical Christian and law professor at Harvard, describes his life as a citizen of these two disparate worlds starkly:

> A lot of my church friends think universities represent the forces of darkness. Law schools—my corner of the academic world—are particularly suspect. A fellow singer in a church choir once asked me what I did for a living. When I told her, she said, "A Christian lawyer? Isn't that sort of like being a Christian prostitute?" She wasn't kidding. . . .
>
> You hear the same kinds of comments running in the other direction. Some years ago, a faculty colleague and I were talking about religion and politics, and this colleague said, "You know, I think you're the first Christian I've ever met who isn't stupid." My professor friend wasn't kidding either.[29]

I think that people of learning and people of faith must talk to one another. Like Bill Stuntz, I see myself as inhabiting both worlds; and we are not alone within universities. A university is, by its nature, pluralistic; and in open, diverse, and democratic societies, faith has insights to contribute.

Any university that banned the study of evolution as improper because of a belief that the world was created ex nihilo by a creator being at a specific time clearly would be both misunderstanding evolution and compromising its status as a university. As a lawyer, I was part of the team that persuaded the Supreme Court that Louisiana's attempt to do just that violated the Constitution. On the other hand, some, in the name of pluralism, would go so far as to drive the faithful from the dialogue, which is not healthy and would result in loss of the conversation's most expansive possibilities.

A 1978 Supreme Court case on a matter other than creationism and evolution is instructive. In *McDaniel v. Paty,* the Court ruled that a Tennessee statute forbidding a member of the clergy from serving in the state legislature was unconstitutional, precisely because the "government may not . . . question whether legislative actions stem from religious conviction."[30] To ban a minister from serving in government for no other reason than that he is visibly a person of faith is as dogmatic as to prohibit stem cell research without presenting any evidence other than the religion of the official doing the banning.

As people of faith enter the public square, it is reasonable to ask that they participate in a way that honors a commitment to reasoned engagement and, indeed, borrows from the challenging dialogue that characterizes our universities. There is no reason to believe that people of faith are incapable of such rigor. In a pluralistic society, public argument must be based on knowledge or reason and subject to inquiry, analysis, and testing. The dialogue must be multilayered, iterative, and extended.

While public officials may begin in a blended position that incorporates religious doctrines, they have an obligation to present and defend their viewpoints on nonreligious grounds. If a conversation that examines those nonreligious grounds reveals them as unpersuasive in public discourse—because extending them convincingly is impossible and simply reasserting them is insufficient—then public officials have no justification for their position.

Even as one who believes in a world of transcendent mysteries and the truths of faith for which there cannot be rational proof, I accept—especially as one who comes out of Catholic triumphalism as I first experienced it—that faith does not bestow a right of imposition. We are free to believe that our God has spoken truth to us, but we do not have the right to impose that truth on those to whom a different God has spoken, or on those who believe there is no god at all. The dogmatism of the unquestioned revealed truth has no place in discourse, whether in the university or the public square.

To accept these propositions is not to deny the importance, let alone existence, of another domain—the domain of faith. It simply is to say that there is no way to reason a person into your faith. Love, which we all accept, shares this quality. Though you can experience a profound love for someone and profess it to him or her, whether he or she reciprocates your love does not turn on arguments well made.

A secular university does not have a role in affirming or undermining faith-based belief. But it does train people not simply for jobs but also for meaningful and useful lives. Questions of meaning remain. Science, technology, and engineering are valued disproportionately against art and the humanities. But as countries seek to build science and technology, they ultimately ask: "How do we nurture creativity?" Similarly, when we begin to see the effects of science and technology on our lives, we ultimately ask: "How do we make sure that we don't debase our souls and disavow our humanity?" It is important that those who inhabit the world of the mind also be open to truths of the spirit.

Conclusion

The sacred space entrusted to those of us who are privileged to live within universities is so precious and so easily undermined that we must promote it actively in word and deed by empowering its participants and expanding its influence.

Here we come back to the danger that a growing secular dogmatism presents to civil discourse. The testing of ideas within the university can serve as a model for reshaping a wider civic dialogue.

The task is daunting, but it is also an essential duty we within the university bear. If we fail to protect the sacred space, we risk the existence of our institutions and the character of our world. So let us look forward by going back to basic principles, accepting the high privilege of not only living in, but also giving renewed life to, the university as sacred space. We *must* do this—at least.

But there is more some of us might choose to do. Once we are convinced that the sacred space itself is safe, we might ask that at least some of our universities move beyond being models of dialogue and counterforces to secular dogmatism; we might ask that they become models of secular ecumenism. This ambitious agenda would require these universities to reconstitute themselves in a new form. In the next part of my argument, I offer a sense of how universities might reconstitute themselves to this end.

3

A University for
an Ecumenical World

Prelude

Just before midnight on Friday, my flight leaves JFK airport in New York for Abu Dhabi. Fourteen hours later, I am in my hotel room near NYU's campus in the Gulf capital. It is ten o'clock on a Saturday evening.

After dinner with friends and a few hours of sleep, I head to my Sunday morning class—Sunday is the first day of the week in the Gulf—with twenty remarkable NYU Abu Dhabi students. Each a story of talent and adventure, they come from eighteen countries, speak, read, and write English well, and have a collective command of nearly thirty other languages. Together, we devote two hours to close analysis of the two hundred pages of unedited Supreme Court opinions they have read for class.

Then, after a break for a quick lunch, I am off to meet my second class of the day—this time, a dozen top students drawn from the three federal Emirati universities. They have been nominated by their schools and selected by NYU faculty to take two courses at NYUAD, one of them mine, for which they get credit in their universities. The syllabus, the same one I use for my NYU Abu Dhabi class in the morning and for a freshman seminar I teach in New York, examines the relationship of government and religion. They, too, have done the reading; now they work with me on the opinions.

Sunday evening is devoted to meetings with colleagues and students. Just before midnight, I am off to the airport for my 2:30 A.M. flight back to New York. I land at 8:00 A.M. Monday and am in my office two hours later.

For the last twelve years, I have repeated this drill about twice a month while school is in session, from the middle of September through early May. Such will be the life of some professors in this new century, a life unimaginable less than a generation ago. It is very different from life in a traditional university.

Every university worthy of the name will be a sacred space for the dialogue that advances thought and understanding. Some universities, however, will go beyond this traditional role to assume a more ambitious office: they will become incubators for a secular ecumenism that not only rejects secular dogmatism but also seeks to create a community of interlocking communities, a whole that is greater than the sum of its parts—a world that today is only a dream. The contours of such a university are already developing; and there is substantial evidence that talented faculty, students, and staff want to be part of it. For many of our great universities, this is the future, and a source of hope.

Globalization as an Axial Moment

Globalization in its economic sense is a defining element of our world. More and more, commerce and communication transcend boundaries, and transactions that used to be merely local now routinely touch multiple continents, implicating multiple legal systems. In this first sense, globalization is ubiquitous and unavoidable, affecting for good and ill governments, markets, and the lives of institutions and citizens everywhere.

Beyond this most common meaning, globalization refers to an even more transformative cultural and societal change that touches the range of human experience, forcing us into relationships with people beyond our borders in unprecedented ways. The infiltration of cultures around the world by American culture is only one example. There are streets in once-remote regions that appear to be transplants from an American suburb, an accelerating homogenization that threatens treasured local traditions. Ironically, as globalization makes us more aware of the rich diversity of societies, it also threatens a loss of that diversity.

Globalization, in this sense, is as much a revolutionary force as its economic counterpart and has as much catalytic potential, positive and negative. In the years ahead, we may witness cultural homogenization—or the opposite. Greater interconnectivity need not destroy diversity. It is up to us whether globalization incorporates and celebrates the wonder of difference, maximizing its benefits while minimizing its costs.

But managing globalization in any of its forms will not be easy. Our ability to do so will depend on our aptitude for reflection, capacity to listen and learn, and willingness to be humble. As we approach a deeper relationship with those who differ from us in important ways, we will need modesty, not certitude—a desire more to discover their truths than to proselytize them. These characteristics do not come naturally in a society increasingly marked by secular dogmatism.

The worldview that inclines some, including me, toward a more optimistic view of globalization is a secular version of the ecumenical approach brought to Catholics like me by Pope John XXIII and the Second Vatican Council. Those made nervous by the religious references should substitute "cosmopolitanism" for ecumenism. Whatever the label, appreciation of this secular ecumenism is indispensable to understanding the full potential of what is unfolding before us.

The great question of our time is how peoples around the world will respond to global compression and the inclusion of unfamiliar elements, drawn invisibly from other cultures, into so many aspects of their familiar, local environment. Some will react out of fear and, responding to the powerful pull of nativism, turn fear to hate. They will narrow their angles of vision, harden traditional patterns of thought, and seek to stem the inflow of the unfamiliar, whether people or ideas. But such gating strategies— economic, political, cultural, or intellectual—will fail. This fortress mentality will escalate tensions between the forces clinging to "the way it was" and those who are carriers of the new and different "way it is becoming." By hunkering down for a battle against the forces of change, those who choose this path will only hasten what some predict will be a "clash of civilizations."

Others will see a tremendous opportunity in the greater connections that result from globalization. They will acknowledge that their own views of the world can be expanded; they will perceive that they have much to learn from others; and they will embrace engagement even with those whose experiences and views are very different from their own. People who carry this spirit of openness and appreciation of community will develop a connection with "the other" and create an age of cultural and intellectual ecumenism.

Of course, there are many others who live joyful and fulfilling lives quite apart from this binary choice. They are good people who choose a life centered in the wonderful enterprise of family and local community. But, they too are affected by the invisible repercussions of how the first two groups I described—the nativists and the ecumenists—work out their starkly different versions of our world.

We—humankind—are at an inflection point, a critical threshold. We soon must choose between the fear that is the currency of populism and the hope that is harbored by those who, like Teilhard de Chardin and my mentor, Ewert Cousins, described the possibility of a Second Axial Age.

In *The Origin and Goal of History*, Karl Jaspers described the period from 800 to 200 B.C.E. as the Axial Age because "it gave birth to everything which, since then, humankind has been able to be."[1] It was the era when Lao-tzu and Confucius revolutionized Chinese thought; Buddha, Mahavira, and the rishis who wrote the Upanishads transformed philosophy, religion, and ethics in India; and the followers of Zoroaster in Persia explored profound questions about the nature of good and evil. In the Levant, Jewish prophets such as Isaiah and Jeremiah sounded calls for higher levels of moral awareness. In Greece, Pythagoras, Socrates, Plato, and Aristotle articulated the fundamental ideas of Western philosophy. Before the Axial Age, the dominant form of consciousness was cosmic, collective, tribal, mythic, and ritualistic. By contrast, the consciousness born in the Axial Age, which was then extended by successor waves such as Christianity, Islam, the Enlightenment, and the scientific revolution, carries a sense of individual identity that permeates the cultures of the world today.

Since the middle of the last century, we have begun to see signs of a Second Axial period. Although first described by theologians, the Second Axial Age also has a progressive, secular dimension. Teilhard predicted a process of "planetization," a shift in the forces of social evolution that he analogized to biological evolution, proceeding from "emergence" and "divergence" to "convergence." The first groupings of humans were familial and tribal, engendering loyalty to a group and separation from other groups. Humanity then diverged, creating different cultures and nations. But the spatial finitude and the spherical shape of our planet were intrinsic constraints: Human beings now occupy all of earth's readily habitable areas, and modern communication and transportation systems mean that groups can no longer detach completely from the world. Instead, humankind is pressed into intimate connection in a planetary community. Even as powerful forces of difference and division turn us against one another, we are being drawn into a global society.

But this global world need not compromise the great gift of experiential diversity. Teilhard saw not a homogenization but rather "creative unions," in which diversity is nurtured and enriched. "In any domain," he wrote, "whether it be the cells of a body, the members of a society, or the elements of a spiritual synthesis—union differentiates."[2] Whether subatomically or globally, elements unite in "center-to-center unions." Just as physics describes centers of mass in the universe that are drawn together, capitals of the world will be connected even more than they are now. They will touch one another at their creative cores, releasing new energy and much deeper understanding. This center-to-center contact offers the promise that we, the citizens of these cities and of this integrated world, may discover what is authentic and vital not only about others but about ourselves.

If we are to realize this promise in the Second Axial Age, a particular style of engagement will be required. The influential ecumenist Raimundo Panikkar, echoing voices as different as Ibn al-'Arabī and Martin Buber, has called it "dialogic dialogue"—as opposed to dialectic dialogue (in which participants seek less to learn from each other than to refute each other's claims). Ewert

Cousins, who first introduced me to Panikkar fifty years ago, before the now-prominent thinker or his Liberation Theology was widely known among theologians in North America or Europe, describes the three phases of dialogic dialogue in spirituality. His analysis can easily be given a secular reading for our emerging global civil society:

> First, the partners meet each other in an atmosphere of mutual understanding, ready to alter misconceptions about each other and eager to appreciate the values of the other. Second, the partners are mutually enriched by passing over into the consciousness of the other so that each can experience the other's values from within the other's perspective. This can be enormously enriching, for often the partners discover in another tradition values which are submerged or only inchoate in their own. It is important at this point to respect the autonomy of the other tradition: in Teilhard's terms, to achieve union in which differences are valued as a basis of creativity. And, third, if such a creative union is achieved, then the [cultures] will have moved into the complexified form of consciousness that will be characteristic of the twenty-first century.[3]

In a May 2008 lecture at the Kennedy Library, British Prime Minister Gordon Brown called on the leaders of the world to seize this ecumenical moment:

> Nothing in President Kennedy's enduring legacy has greater importance now—at the beginning of the twenty-first century—than his words on your

Independence Day in 1962, when he proposed a global declaration of interdependence. . . . So, if the 1776
Declaration of Independence stated a self-evident
truth (that we are all created equal) JFK's Declaration
of Interdependence in 1962 added another self-
evident truth: that we are all of us—all of us throughout the world—in this together. Each of us our
brother's keeper, each of us, to quote Martin Luther
King, part of an inescapable web of mutuality.[4]

Prime Minister Brown continued: "To adapt an aphorism
of President Kennedy, the new frontier is that there is no
frontier—no frontier for the Internet, for the mobile phone,
for e-mails, for the cyber-world; no frontier for the capacity of
individuals to influence, inform or even infuriate each other.
And because times are new we must—in Robert Kennedy's
words—think anew. We must, as he said, leave behind yesterday
and embrace tomorrow."[5]

While in President Kennedy's time foreign relations were
founded almost exclusively on the relative power of governments, today we must recognize the relevance to foreign policy
of what we see before our eyes—that everywhere around us
people are forming global associations, global connections, and
global communities; that all over the world, from culture to
education to social action, individuals are harnessing people
power to transcend states, for good and sometimes for ill. And
they are compelling institutions and authorities to follow their
example, with regulators, environmental and development
agencies, militaries, law enforcement, and judges all having to
cooperate directly across frontiers.

This Teilhardian, ecumenical, cosmopolitan worldview may
seem quite naïve, especially given recent political developments.

Despite the darkening forces buffeting us, however, I believe that the achievement of this affirmative vision is possible—and that universities have an essential role in fostering its development. The question then becomes: In the vast span of time, do I believe, to paraphrase Martin Luther King, that the arc of progress bends toward a morally better place and a more integrated world? The answer is that I do. And I draw hope from the fact that a secular version of ecumenism ought to be easier to realize than the theological version I have seen develop into a mature reality over the last sixty years.

I also draw hope from my daily experiences in New York City, arguably the world's first ecumenical city, a community both global and local. In 1609, Amsterdam was home to the most progressive and culturally diverse society in Europe. Small, but remarkably vital and adventurous, Amsterdam was the source of half the world's published books throughout the seventeenth century and sent expeditions to uncharted waters and lands unknown to Europeans. When Henry Hudson, on one of those expeditions, sailed into New York harbor for the Dutch East India Company, he encountered an island that centuries later would become a global hub of commerce and ideas, its influence reaching much farther than even the most ambitious of his voyages.

Reflecting these origins, New Amsterdam would become New York, the urban prototype for the American experiment— open to immigrants, enriched by many cultures, always striving. In his marvelous history of Dutch Manhattan, Russell Shorto reports that New Amsterdam was restless, ambitious, and polyglot: "It was Manhattan right from the start."

Today, nearly 40 percent of the city's citizens were born outside the United States.[6] One hundred and forty languages heard on the streets of New York are the first languages of the person speaking them.[7] Remarkably, in each enclave in this city of interlocking cultures, where communities maintain the food, music, and language of the "old country," the people walking the streets think of each other and themselves as, first and foremost, New Yorkers. New York is not perfect, but it does provide a glimpse of the world that could be.

If we bet against ourselves, if we say that the headwinds we face—which are undeniably strong, perhaps even at major storm levels—do not admit progress, and if we then stop fighting for the vision that might be, there will be no progress. The only way to have hope is to have faith. It is out of that faith that I choose to be an optimist.

What we do know is that if we are to shape the forces of globalization for the good, we will have to embrace difference, understanding, and dialogue. As we build an interconnected world, every one of us must accept a responsibility for the wellness of every other being, to the extent that we can effect it. Each of us must not only extend receptivity and care to those in our immediate community of belonging. We must also reach beyond our immediate community to the people of the many other communities in our miniaturized world.

In the struggle against the powerful forces of nativism and ethnocentrism and on behalf of a new Axial consciousness, universities are well equipped to provide the infrastructure for a world that honors difference. Universities are the homes of the search for understanding. As we have seen, they are instruments of dialogue—resisting isolation and divisiveness, and inviting difficult conversations. They specialize in patient encounters with difference, with what is unknown or other. And they live the belief that through such encounters, new modes of knowing develop. They know the dangers of certitude and silencing, and are profoundly aware of the lethal nature of intellectual homogenization and party lines, in conversation or within disciplines.

Beyond this, universities have a special capacity to study the causes, effects, and unintended consequences of globalization. There is no better venue than the university to raise the consciousness of a transforming world about both the obvious and unknown ramifications of these trends.

Our universities are equipped to be objective evaluators, offering analysis of such critical issues as social equity, fundamental fairness, and the transparency of society's institutions and structures. They can lead a serious conversation about moral consequences. They can identify, weigh, and critique decision makers' compromises and priorities. They can protect heterogeneity. And, they can stand apart from the "market world" at this moment when the market threatens to become a measure of all things. In short, universities can become the watchdogs of society, the issue spotters of the global era, posing questions and choices for society and demanding coherent, defensible answers from those who are responsible for public policy.

But universities are not only observers of the world; they are daily participants in it. The standards by which they evaluate the performance of others must be the measure of their own conduct. Universities themselves must be responsible global citizens.

Universities, Idea Capitals, and the New Cosmopolitans

Urban universities and colleges have a special advantage in contributing to the infrastructure of an ecumenical world. They draw their life force from their surroundings, the cities that house and nurture them, reservoirs of intellectual and cultural talent. They have a common institutional DNA, reflecting what I call the "locational endowment"—a concentration of mind (talent) and matter (infrastructure), an entrepreneurial spirit, an embrace of complexity and openness, a connection to the world beyond walls. Many of the best urban universities are literally without walls. Like NYU, they are "in and of the city." Indeed, NYU is a powerful example of how, in this globalized world, a university and its city can reinforce one another.

New York was relatively small in 1831, when NYU was founded. With a modest population of two hundred thousand, it only recently had surpassed Philadelphia to become the largest city in the country. The United States was still an agrarian society; above what is now 14th Street, Manhattan was farmland. Initially, the city's downtown sector was a gateway for importing, manufacturing, and distributing goods. When other cities exceeded it as a port and manufacturing center, New York transformed its downtown, becoming the nation's preeminent location for new forms of commerce in three industries: finance, insurance, and real estate—what came to be called the FIRE sector of the economy.

Like the earlier gateway economy, the FIRE sector flourished, and New York flourished with it. In an economy fueled by the stock market, businesses found real opportunity in being situated near the prime trading floor, allowing them to conduct daily, and even hourly, transactions. Insurance followed finance, and real estate thrived.

Today, because of the internet, physical proximity to related businesses is no longer the magnet it was. The number of jobs in finance, insurance, and real estate has declined—down by more than 10 percent in the last thirty years.[8] Executives routinely conduct business from Aspen or make deals from the

Caribbean. They plan their lives and determine the location of their businesses accordingly. In response, New York has reinvented itself once again, supplementing its traditional strength in FIRE by developing strength in a new trilogy—ICE, the intellectual, cultural, and educational sectors. Universities are at the center of this combined FIRE and ICE strategy.

There are more college students in New York than in any other American city. New York is the academic capital of the world in fields as diverse as philosophy, math, law, and film. This concentration of intellectual activity is vividly evident in science: 132 living Nobel laureates; 146 members of the National Academy of Sciences; the highest number of science students and postdocs; 11 major academic medical research institutions; and 5 biology PhD programs.[9]

New York State has built upon New York City's strength. Among American students, New York State is the leading destination (gross and net) among the fifty states for freshmen who leave their home state for college. New York is home to more of the top one hundred colleges and universities than any other state.[10] And seven of New York's medical schools rank among the nation's top fifty.[11]

In 2008, Prime Minister Gordon Brown and I spoke about the connections among universities, the FIRE and ICE sectors, and the emergence of a network of idea capitals around the world.

"Being part of such an integrated, networked world is a natural move for universities," I told him, "because universities have always operated beyond sovereignty." For a thousand years, the ideas and learning generated by universities have crossed borders and languages.

He took out a pad and said, "I'm going to write that down and use it. I love the notion of thinking beyond sovereignty."

"Mr. Prime Minister," I responded, "it seems to me that it's one thing for John, president of a university, to use the phrase 'beyond sovereignty.' But it's quite another for the head of a government to use it."

To which he replied: "You're wrong. The forces you describe will inevitably knit together this network of idea capitals. And it is the task of Britain's leader to plan so that London is a main stop."

A lot of water has flowed under the bridge, including Brexit for the UK and the 2016 election in the United States of a president seemingly committed to dismantling the infrastructure of the interconnected world that America worked hard to build since the end of World War II. We have seen the rise of an isolationism we could not have imagined in 2008. Nevertheless, I have faith that, viewed over time, it will become clear that Prime Minister Brown was right when he said that a networked set of idea capitals will attract the talent and hope of the world. Whether one believes our time is Axial or not, the greatest population centers of the future will be driven less by production and more by the ideas and innovation of their most creative global citizens. The universities and the environments they create around them will be the magnets attracting these talented people.

Of course, universities are not the only element of the ICE sector that combines with the traditional FIRE sector to create an "idea capital." In New York and in the two dozen other major idea capitals around the world, great universities combine with other cultural and artistic institutions: museums, libraries, theaters, concert halls, studios, and galleries. But strong universities are the essence of the ICE sector. As Daniel Patrick Moynihan put it when he was asked how he would create a world class city: "Create a great university—and wait."

Who will populate these idea capitals?

When asked where he was from, the fourth-century B.C.E. Greek philosopher Diogenes of Sinope is famously said to have replied, "I am a citizen of the world"—a *kosmopolitis*. He meant that he was not limited by the biases of place. In the original Greek context, cosmopolitans valued treating people, no matter who they were or where they were born, as if they were siblings whose claims on care and fairness were grounded in the fact that they were all human beings.

Over millennia, thinkers from Confucius to Socrates to Ibn al-'Arab to Petrarch to Kant have invoked cosmopolitanism as fundamental to society. Later, the term developed a secondary meaning—to be cultured or sophisticated. But it continues to signify a person who is a citizen of the world and who sees others through a wider frame. A cosmopolitan maintains a sense of place, country, ethnicity, religion, and culture, even while embracing, respecting, learning from, and adapting to global diversity. That is, a cosmopolitan is ecumenical.

My NYU colleague Kwame Anthony Appiah has named these new leaders of society "cosmopolitan patriots."[12]

> The cosmopolitan patriot can entertain the possibility of a world in which everyone is a rooted cosmopolitan, attached to a home of his or her own, with its own cultural particularities, but taking pleasure from the presence of other, different places that are home to other, different, people.
>
> The cosmopolitan also imagines that in such a world not everyone will find it best to stay in their natal patria, so that the circulation of people among different localities will involve not only cultural tourism (which the cosmopolitan admits to enjoying)

> but migration, nomadism, diaspora. . . . [T]hese pro-
> cesses have too often been the result of forces we
> should deplore; the old migrants were often refugees,
> and older diasporas often began in an involuntary
> exile. But what can be hateful if coerced can be cele-
> brated when it flows from the free decisions of indi-
> viduals or of groups.[13]

In a world of cosmopolitan patriots, people would accept the citizens' responsibility to nurture the culture and the politics of their homes. Many would spend their lives in the places that shaped them, which is one of the reasons local cultural practices would be sustained and transmitted. But others would move, their cultural practices traveling with them, as they always have. The result would be a world in which each local form of human life was the culmination of persistent processes of cultural hybridization—a world much like the one we live in now.

Increasingly, the cosmopolitans will be attracted to places that accommodate the global lives they wish to lead. They will be drawn to idea capitals and will offer the attitude and talent to sustain them. There have always been idea capitals, but their influence was local or regional. In contrast, the interchange among the idea capitals of this century will be global. Just as philosophers and artists moved among Milan, Venice, Florence, and Rome during the Italian Renaissance, so in the decades to come thought leaders and their ideas will circulate among Abu Dhabi, London, New York, Shanghai, and other key cities. As my colleague Richard Florida has argued, the world taking shape is a world that is "spiky" rather than flat, with talent, resources, and opportunities clustered in specific locations. In his view, globalization is not leveling the playing field but redrawing it so that places that attract a disproportionate share of the world's creative capacity will have the brightest future.

This process is already well begun. By 2050, the world's capitals of creativity will have emerged. Some candidates are obvious, because of their current pools of talent, but complacency or lack of vision may cause even the well-positioned to squander opportunity. No city will become one of tomorrow's idea capitals by heritage or accident. That attainment will require both vision and effort. If leaders around the world want to shape the future, not simply react to it or be its observers, they will nurture the creative sector.

At NYU, we saw the city's allure early on as we used our location in New York to attract talented faculty. Even in an increasingly specialized academic world, the most intellectually energetic colleagues want to live in an environment that is as alive as they are. Leading genomicists want to talk not only to other great genomicists but also to great philosophers, political scientists, and scholars of literature and the arts. They want to listen to a world-class orchestra and attend an acclaimed ballet or play. They also want these encounters and experiences for their families. What we found to be true for university faculty members is also true for those who work in any talent enterprise: The most talented among us want to live among the most talented among us, and not only in their fields. The cosmopolitans want to live with other cosmopolitans in the idea capitals they create by their presence.

A University Model for an Ecumenical World

Of the eighty-five institutions that exist today as they did five hundred years ago, seventy are universities.[14] Universities have always been the incubators of measured, deliberate advancement, preserving the wisdom and knowledge of the past as they challenge orthodoxy. Over the centuries, the structure of our great universities has evolved, but for most of this period it has evolved slowly.

The American university in its traditional form is still the global standard. Rankings are always problematic and imprecise, but for many years and across various measures, universities in the United States have dominated the rankings of international universities. In most, seven of the top ten and over forty of the top fifty are American centers of research and learning.

The traditional university has been defined in important ways by location. Most are located in one place and view themselves in relation to that place. But as the world has become more intimate and the effects of globalization more pronounced, a subtle but fundamental transformation of the operation and structure of several great universities has occurred—one that will become more marked in the decades ahead.

Whether politically palatable or not, universities increasingly operate beyond sovereignty. As Sir Nigel Thrift, vice chancellor of Warwick University and later director of the Schwarzman Scholars program, has put it:

> Universities across the world are facing the challenge of globalizing trends in student demand and research funding by internationalizing their operations both at home and abroad. The challenges are easier to meet at home, where established modes of mobility and diversity can quickly be accelerated. This important work—opening our institutional cultures to worlds beyond the local and national cultures in which universities as institutional presences are suspended—is both a challenging and

long-term endeavor. But domestic policy on internationalization, safely judged within local confines,
is the relatively easy bit; it is "internationalization
light," in other words, or diversity very much on
our own terms.

Abroad, the challenges are altogether of a different magnitude and are much more compelling.
Research-intensive universities have a crucial role to
play in the knowledge economies of the global era—
driving innovation, creating sustainable change,
educating global citizens, and tackling in collaborative endeavors the problems that bedevil our planet.
Yet today very few universities can claim either a
global presence or possess the sets of relationships
that will allow them to be as effective as we will need
universities to be in coming decades.[15]

In a letter to the Yale community, then-President Rick
Levin and his provost, Peter Salovey (now Yale's president),
urged an aggressive response to these challenges: "It is inevitable that the world's leading universities by the middle of this
century will have international campuses. If [universities] are
to serve the world as successfully in the 21st century as we have
served our nation in the 20th, a greater global presence will be
required."[16]

Arthur Levine, president of the Woodrow Wilson Fellowship Foundation, warned those who would be tempted to take
a cautious, modest approach: "Some bold universities will lead.
Others will be popularizers. And others will hold onto the past
and will be destined to fail."[17]

Whether a major institutional response by our universities
is as imperative as these commentators claim—and I believe it

is—there will be a wide range of responses to the interconnectivity that characterizes our world, with no single "right" way.

Some great universities will choose to continue along their current path of accomplishment and take only minimal measures to respond to the forces of globalization. No doubt, a few that choose this approach will continue to attract very talented faculty and students, choosing to maintain traditions of excellence with proven methods. The universities that make this choice will accept a loss of talent or access to ideas that follows from such traditionalism. The best, some of which have been among the world's leading universities for generations, will remain great places decades from now.

Another set of universities will adopt a slightly—but only slightly—more aggressive strategy: They will continue to do what they have been doing, at the same time working a bit harder to create meaningful international possibilities through more elaborate student exchange programs, occasional visits from scholars, and collaboration across national boundaries in various disciplines. Almost a century ago, some schools began to make it possible for their students to study elsewhere for a semester or more. Today, nearly every university allows it, even though some maintain structural barriers that make it difficult to do so. In the future, universities will pay more attention to such study-away opportunities and to creating a more global experience on campus by encouraging a greater presence of international scholars—although those that choose this second model will often view these initiatives as a welcome but not essential enhancement of their curriculum and research.

Still other universities will choose a third model, a more aggressive version of the second, in which universities enter a formal network of alliances with partner universities to permit the movement of students and perhaps faculty, much like the code-share systems used by airline alliances. This approach will enable those who want to participate more fully in a global flow of ideas to enjoy more significant study and research opportunities away from a home campus, while relying on the partner institutions to maintain quality and integration of courses taken "away" with the requirements mandated by the student's home program.

There are very good reasons that universities might choose one of these three models. Some may place a lower priority on the factors that, for me, are the predicate for incorporating the ecumenical spirit into the structure and ethos of the university. Others may be committed to values that run counter to sending students away from campus. Still others might be constrained by political factors (public universities that must answer to the regents and legislators who fund them, or universities that must answer to alumni who have a more traditional view of their alma mater). A final group might be limited by financial factors, such as a loss of revenue while students are away.

As the American Council on Education's 2012 Report of the Blue Ribbon Panel on Global Engagement put it: "Specific forms of collaboration will vary; each institution will have to consider its specific mission, aspirations, and capacities for establishing partnerships and being a good partner. In this context, and given ACE's traditional role, it is important that the Council guide and assist American colleges and universities in responding to the imperative strategically and substantively with a globalized higher education environment and interconnected world."[18]

While understanding that the choice for many universities may be one of the first three models I have described, we come now to a fourth model, one that embraces the arguments I have made about the global flow of ideas and talent. This model seeks to create within the university both attitudinal and structural changes to encourage that flow, even as it seeks to hold true to those characteristics that have made great universities the magnificent institutions they are: intellectual rigor, open inquiry, merit review, academic freedom, and a broad range of disciplinary interests.

Since about 2000, in no small part with my encouragement, NYU has pursued this fourth approach. My extraordinary successor, Andrew Hamilton, who came to NYU after leading Oxford University for seven years, has made it clear that NYU will continue to move in this direction; an ecumenical spirit is in the nature of NYU and its first home, New York City. What follows is not a prediction of what NYU will be like. The point, rather, is that the success of what NYU already has built is sufficient proof that an organic global university can be created. For this reason, it is worth examining its features in detail.

The Architecture of NYU's Global Network University

NYU's evolution into the global network university model flows naturally from its history and character. As a university located in one of the great cosmopolitan cities of the world, NYU affirms the significance of place to its mission and to the lives and work of its faculty and students. In its nearly two hundred years, NYU has been defined by its relationship to New York City and the spirit it embodies.

Today, New York City is a miniaturization of the world. In its schools, every nation is represented by a child who was born in that country. In the city's neighborhoods, a visitor can hear the languages, songs, and prayers of the world—and can taste the food of every nation. New Yorkers struggle with the issues that divide them; but, in the end, they work to create a Second Axial Age "community of communities."

NYU shares not just the city's geography but its consciousness and character. Like New York, NYU is an extremely cacophonous, complex organism. It does not define itself by traditionally unifying university activities such as sports. In a strange twist, the unifying element of the university is its complexity—and the challenge and opportunity such complexity offers in teaching the skills of finding community in an environment that makes it hard to find.

The university has built its program around this reality. Its residence halls feature aggregations of students on "exploration floors," bringing together those with passions for chess, dance, jazz, crosswords, food—nearly fifty possibilities, led by resident faculty mentors. The floors give students the skills of building a small community and then connecting from that base to communities beyond their own. Student visits to New York City's neighborhoods emphasize the variety of the world's peoples. Then, prepared by these experiences, students are urged to spend semesters at NYU's study-away sites. NYU sends more students to study away than any other university, and many students spend two or three semesters away from the campus they call home. NYU, always in and of the city, is now in and of the world.

The ramifications of this move are still being absorbed, but there are already three characteristics illustrated by NYU's approach that likely will be a part of this fourth model as it evolves at NYU and elsewhere. Universities that choose this direction will be global, they will be a network, and they will be organic. This model is not a hub-and-spoke or branch-campus system. It is an organic circulatory system through which faculty and students move without impediment, advancing their research and studies as easily as they would if they were moving among buildings on campus. By avoiding the impediments to mobility—the systemic sclerosis—associated with other models, this circulation both helps ensure quality and captures unique academic advantages.

The fundamental organizational element of NYU's global network university is the portal campus, a point of primary affiliation and activity, with the capacity to accommodate fully its faculty and students. Such a campus grants degrees. If students wish, they may complete an entire program of study in this single setting, without visiting any other part of the system. However, each NYU portal is very much connected to the other two, building on the assets of the others. Today, NYU is anchored in three carefully chosen, comprehensive "portal campuses"—New York, Abu Dhabi, and Shanghai.

New York remains home to most of the university's faculty, students, and staff. It houses a greater variety and depth of program in most areas than the two other portal campuses. Even so, the campuses in Abu Dhabi and Shanghai house a wide range of curricular and research programs, supported at the highest levels of excellence, including some not available at the New York campus.

The three portal campuses are complemented by eleven "study-away sites" on six continents. Each of these sites is integrated into the academic mission and program of the portal campuses. Each offers, in addition to basic academic courses, opportunities that derive from the distinctive environment of the site. For example, the Accra site emphasizes global public health and the economics of development; NYU Berlin, art and the humanities; NYU Prague, music, global media, and political transition; and NYU Sydney, the environment, native cultures, and film. These sites attract faculty and students who are interested in the campus's specialty and see value in being in context, but they also appeal to those who are intrigued by new experiences.

The system is designed for mobility. Each study-away site offers enough basic courses to allow students to complete core requirements, even—at specified sites—in track programs such as engineering, science, business, or film. All courses at any site are approved by the relevant department at the New York campus, and count just as if they were offerings in New York. The sites are also venues for conferences, lectures, research, and, in some places, graduate programs culminating in a degree. As such, they provide deep connections between NYU and the academic and intellectual communities of the cities where the sites are located.

Although study away has traditionally focused on juniors and seniors, some study-away sites now have programs for entering college freshmen. We have discovered that many entering students prefer to begin their studies at a site, moving to New York for their second year, then studying at other sites in the network in their third year, before returning to New York for their senior year. One recent graduate who completed his NYU bachelor's degree in four years enjoyed five study-away semesters.

Schools and units that use the sites optimally can develop new programs to enhance the curriculum. For example, NYU's undergraduate business school has allowed students to do five semesters in New York, one in London, one in Shanghai, and one in Buenos Aires—all with professors selected by NYU, courses developed by NYU, and quality at the level NYU demands. The result is a highly enriched business curriculum that better prepares its students for today's business environment. Similar programs, fully integrated with their respective academic majors, exist or are being developed in most of NYU's units, with courses that meet all degree requirements. And, using technology, it is also possible to offer courses at one site that include students who are at other locations, enabling an exploration of what is universal and what is particular to a specific local setting.

Notably, the global network university does not preempt the creation of special-purpose sites when there is a strong academic justification for such a site and when the academic advantages of running an "out-of-system" site would otherwise not be available. For example, NYU made provision for several archeological digs. Such special purpose sites operate as they would in any university structure; they do not involve the commitment of ancillary services that are routine at study-away sites (such as dorms, extracurricular activities, internships, or counseling).

This structure was not born in an instant, but was a full five decades in the making. NYU's first formal initiatives outside the United States began with study-away sites in Madrid in 1959 and Paris in 1969, originally exclusively for Spanish and French majors but later broadened to include other students. By 2000, NYU had launched additional study-away sites in Florence and London and had begun encouraging students to seriously consider a semester away at one of these four campuses. Then two realities came into focus. First, the study-away program was wholly Eurocentric. Second, only about 7 percent of NYU students were going abroad for even a semester, and the largest groups that did were language majors. For a university rooted in the spirit of New York, such a situation was unacceptable.

Over the next five years, new study-away sites were added in Accra, Berlin, Buenos Aires, Prague, Shanghai, Sydney, Tel Aviv, and Washington, DC. By 2005, our growing understanding of NYU's relationship to globalization and its emerging civil society prompted the realization that the Arab and Muslim world—one-quarter of the world's people and a repository of a distinguished intellectual and cultural history—was missing from the picture.

We considered several possible study-away sites, but almost everyone we consulted said that both the leadership and culture of Abu Dhabi in the United Arab Emirates made it the right choice. The more we came to know Abu Dhabi, the more we appreciated it as an emerging idea capital. Three-quarters of the world's countries are represented among those who reside in Abu Dhabi. And about the same number of languages are spoken there as in New York. Like New York, Abu Dhabi is a welcoming city—reflecting the Bedouin culture of hospitality upon which it is built. This, coupled with Abu Dhabi's high-quality leadership and its ambition, made it the most attractive option.

So it was that in 2006 the provost constituted a faculty committee to do its own analysis and advise us on what issues they thought we should clarify before moving forward to an agreement. The chair of the committee was the then-chair of the Faculty Senators' Council. The committee advised that we proceed, subject to gaining assurances that NYU would have complete control over academic, curricular, admissions, and hiring decisions—and that the core principle of academic freedom would prevail on the new campus. Over the following six months, our Abu Dhabi partners agreed to all of these conditions.

As conversations with Abu Dhabi advanced, they went well beyond the original modest possibility of locating a study-away site there to the idea of a comprehensive campus that would function like NYU New York, although smaller. With the notion of a global network university now coming into focus, this new campus could be designed to attract some of the most talented students in the world, who after entering the university via the Abu Dhabi portal could move through the global network for up to three study-away semesters.

The origin of NYU Shanghai was different, yet mirrored in many ways the experience in Abu Dhabi. By 2010, NYU had operated successfully for several years a study-away site in Shanghai, building meaningful connections with Shanghai's educational and governmental leaders. Through these connections, they came to know NYU, our plans for a global network university, and the success of the campus in Abu Dhabi. This led them to broach with NYU the possibility of opening a third portal campus in their city.

This new NYU portal campus started with the same indispensable foundation as NYU Abu Dhabi—partners who believed in the value of education, understood and prized the liberal arts and science educational tradition, viewed their city as an idea capital and center of commerce, shared a vision of global education, and recognized how potent it might be to introduce a gateway in Shanghai to a global network university.

By 2015, NYU New York, NYU Abu Dhabi, and NYU Shanghai were mature portal campuses in a global network university. In retrospect, two early decisions were important to the ultimate success of these ventures: First, the commitment that the new undergraduate campuses would be liberal arts colleges; and, second, the commitment that the degrees conferred in Abu Dhabi and Shanghai would be full NYU degrees.

It is noteworthy that both partners—the governments of Abu Dhabi and Shanghai—sought in NYU a partner to create an undergraduate college in the liberal arts tradition. This commitment signaled at the outset that those involved appreciated traditional standards of excellence, even as they sought to break new ground.

The case for liberal arts education is that it broadens and balances the mind. The sweep and plasticity of the curriculum impart an intellectual nimbleness and expand angles of vision that help make life's transitions springboards rather than disruptions. The case for building this kind of undergraduate liberal arts education within a research university is that there is great reward in exposing students, even as they begin their learning, to professors who are not only masters of current knowledge but also creators of tomorrow's knowledge. Ideally, the undergraduates also participate in the creative process.

These arguments are powerfully persuasive to those who have experienced the magic that happens when these ideals are realized. Still, even our best universities often fail to integrate most undergraduates into the research enterprise. It is relatively rare for the most advanced researchers to engage undergraduates in the classroom, which makes it harder for undergraduates to connect with the advanced research that is being done on campus. From the beginning, those creating the campuses in NYU Abu Dhabi and NYU Shanghai were committed to the maximum possible realization of the ideal. This was a very positive indicator—especially in times when political leaders around the globe are increasingly shaping higher education policy on narrow, utilitarian principles.

The second factor contributing to the success of NYU's ventures in Abu Dhabi and Shanghai was that the degrees conferred were and are full NYU degrees. Some contended that by offering degrees in distant places away from the "main" campus NYU would see the dilution of standards and its "brand." The truth has been quite the opposite. By putting an NYU degree at stake, the team that created these portal campuses ensured that every academic element of the campuses would meet the highest standards, because the guarantors of quality—the deans, faculty, and academic leaders—would be vigilant in protecting the quality of the degree.

The commitment to safeguarding quality—in everything from faculty appointments to admissions to curriculum—is amplified by the circulation of faculty and students throughout the network. Indeed, conceptualizing the global network as a circulatory system rather than as a federation of branch campuses turns out to be a key factor in maintaining academic quality. As one very senior New York–based faculty member put it: "If those students over there, prepared by faculty in courses over there, are going to arrive in my class, I am going to pay attention to what is going on over there and who is doing it." She did. As did other lead faculty. And the level of quality attained at both campuses went beyond what anyone had imagined was attainable.

Nothing in the architecture of the global network university requires NYU, or any university that chooses this model, to abandon consortia (such as the League of World Universities or Universitas 21) or other supplementary programs that provide study-away or research opportunities. On the contrary, NYU has hundreds of these arrangements; the global network university has made such cooperation easier and more effective. So, if an NYU faculty member or student would prefer to move outside of the NYU network to spend time at any of the many partner institutions with which the university has such an agreement, he or she is free to do so.

Most NYU students choose to remain within the network, however, because there are significant advantages to doing so. The portal campuses and study-away sites are fully integrated. Academic work completed in one location can be used as the basis for progress at another, and integrated technology makes it easy for researchers and students in the various locations to

work with each other. The network also offers seamless connectivity with the library, administrative support systems, linked
databases, and health and wellness services.

Although the network's technological backbone is important, it is not a substitute for personal interaction. An advantage
of the global network university is that, even as new technology magnifies connections and communication among those
in the network, the network itself offers continuous opportunities to interact in person. Important insights often come in
conversation over a cup of coffee. The robust dialogue that has
characterized American higher education and engaged students
as active participants in learning depends in large part on the
alchemy of personal contact. For this, it is important that students and faculty are together on campus. Meanwhile, technology plays a supportive, not a controlling, role.

Because portal campuses and study-away sites are a permanent presence in important idea capitals and because the
university becomes part of the local intellectual and academic
landscape, the university's citizens enjoy greater access to local
schools, workplaces, governments, research centers, museums,
businesses, and community agencies. These connections provide signature NYU experiences such as community service
and internships.

The effect of a fully operating network of this sort can be
kaleidoscopic. A professor in New York or Abu Dhabi or Shanghai can offer a course to students at several sites. As part of the
course, he or she could assign team exercises, with students
from different sites tasked to work together in sets. That assign-
ment could foster deeper insight, but in a global network, it
might be only the start of a continuing relationship among
participants. Some or all of the teamed students might decide
to get together during the following semester or year, gathering

to study away for a semester at a particular site. Groupings of students might form, dissipate, and then reconstitute in various combinations and places.

The global network builds naturally on the way academic disciplines already operate. The most advanced research often depends on international collaboration. Leading researchers work with collaborators and coauthors around the world. The network extends this practice by building it into the structure of the university. As faculty and students circulate through the system, they gain not only from the unique attributes of each location, but also from the experience of moving from site to site and the modes of cooperation that develop naturally in such a constantly changing environment.

NYU long has used the wonderful "locational endowment" of Greenwich Village and New York City to draw talent it might not otherwise have enticed to join it. Now, it has a unique global structural endowment: The global network and the mobility it facilitates are an added lure, drawing the talented faculty and student who are the lifeblood of the university.

NYU Abu Dhabi and NYU Shanghai as Proof of Concept

In 2006, as the leadership of Abu Dhabi and NYU conceptualized the partnership that created NYU Abu Dhabi, they set ambitious goals. They hoped to attract academic leaders and students who were as outstanding as those at the world's finest universities. A decade later, even those expectations seem modest compared to what has happened.

The initial NYU team leader was one of New York's deans, who moved to Abu Dhabi with her husband and young children. The successful president of one of America's leading liberal arts

colleges left that institution to become the inaugural vice chancellor. The head of a major initiative in genomics in New York
moved to Abu Dhabi, co-locating his lab, to be the campus
provost. And so it was that from admissions to public safety to
student life to technology, many of the very best faculty and
staff joined the project with enthusiasm. A decade later, most
are still part of it.

Those who chose to come had a range of motivations.
Some faculty were drawn by the mission and the opportunity
to build a curriculum from scratch, such as the innovative science curriculum that was unencumbered by the obstacles associated with reforming an existing structure. Others were
attracted by research interests, as was the case with a Middle
Eastern studies professor, whose hope, now realized, was to
solicit and organize definitive translations of major Arabic
works, or the linguistic neuroscientist who was interested in
the languages of the region.

From the beginning, NYU Abu Dhabi was envisioned as
a research university, with all that implies, into which a liberal
arts college would be fully integrated. Beginning in 2007, three
years before the first freshman arrived, the NYU Abu Dhabi team
set out to recruit faculty. Some of the faculty for the new campus
would circulate periodically from among existing faculty at NYU
New York. Others would be selected by the departments or units
in New York to be in Abu Dhabi most of the time. Together, they
would develop the liberal arts curriculum of the new campus.
That same year, some of NYU's lead faculty began research
projects in Abu Dhabi that operated jointly with work being
conducted in New York. And leading faculty from New York
organized conferences in Abu Dhabi—several dozen each year—
that spanned the disciplines. By September 2010, when the first
undergraduates arrived, there was already a well-established

culture of advanced academic research, and faculty teams committed to teaching and mentoring the incoming class had already
implemented the foundations of the new curriculum.

Not surprisingly, the groundbreaking undergraduate
opportunity in Abu Dhabi appealed to a high-talent group of
students. The admissions team sought a cohort—literally from
around the globe—who were "clearly admissible, on the traditional norms, to ANY college or university in the world." But, from
the start, they understood that finding students who met this
standard alone would not be enough. Each admitted student had
to manifest a disposition to cosmopolitanism that revealed a commitment to creating a global community that relished diversity.

The goal in the first year was to open with a hundred such
students. Since the most successful liberal arts colleges in the
United States enjoyed a 60 percent yield on their offers of
admission—that is, 60 percent of those applicants who were
offered a spot in the class chose to attend—the team sought 180
candidates worthy of offers.

From that very first year, the results have been astonishing.
For the inaugural class, just two percent of the applicants were
offered admission—fewer than two hundred out of over nine
thousand applicants. Those pioneers came from thirty-nine
countries and spoke forty-three languages. Nearly 90 percent
were at least bilingual. Their SAT verbal scores stood at 770 at
the class's 75th percentile, and their math scores were at 780 at
the 75th percentile—scores matching the most highly selective
universities in the world. A remarkable 79 percent who were
offered spots in the class accepted, a higher percentage than
even the most selective liberal arts colleges in the United States
and comparable to the percentages at the very best universities.
Students in that first cohort declined offers from eight of the
top ten liberal arts colleges in the United States and eighteen of

the top twenty-five research universities. In that very first year, NYU Abu Dhabi established itself as one of the world's most selective undergraduate colleges and, arguably, the first truly global university.

As attractive as Abu Dhabi and the opportunities for learning there may have been to this initial group, the critical factor in their choice of NYU Abu Dhabi was the prospect of working with peers who shared a cosmopolitan (in Appiah's sense) view of the world—not only in Abu Dhabi but at the other campuses of the global network university. For all the advantages of NYU Abu Dhabi, if it were a traditional university rather than a portal in a global network university, it would not have appealed as strongly as it did to these students. Over the four years, all but two of that first class spent at least a full semester studying away; the average student visited ten countries as part of his or her academic experience; and even as they lived this cosmopolitan life, over a third published academic work, 85 percent of them held internships, and 70 percent did community service.

The NYU Abu Dhabi class has grown in size (to approximately four hundred in the latest entering class), but the quality of that first group of arrivals has been maintained. In fact, by the customary indicators, the quality of each succeeding class has increased. And the careful work of the admissions team is now manifest in four sets of graduates whose achievements are staggering. With a total of fewer than fifteen hundred graduates in these classes, there are ten Rhodes Scholars and dozens of other major award winners, no doubt in significant part due to the deep engagement of the students with the research of leading faculty. And, remarkably, virtually all of the students who entered in fall of 2010 graduated from NYU Abu Dhabi in the spring of 2014. Students who had come from every corner of the world stayed right through the four years, thrived, and left with a love for their college and Abu Dhabi.

Like NYU Abu Dhabi, NYU Shanghai is a research university with a fully integrated liberal arts college. But its distinction is that the campus is both bicultural and multicultural: 50 percent of its students are Chinese, with the other 50 percent from outside of China. But the standard for faculty and students is the same as in Abu Dhabi—only the highest level of achievement by all traditional measures, combined with a serious commitment to building a cosmopolitan community at the university and in the world. For example, all the admitted Chinese students in the inaugural class not only scored in the very top tier (1 percent) on the test taken by over 9 million high school students (the level required by the "C9," China's elite schools), but also passed muster after two days of classes and interviews by the NYU Shanghai admissions team confirmed their commitment to creating a global community.

Faculty from NYU New York sought to be involved, and outstanding faculty from other universities joined the NYU Shanghai team. Of course, the faculty, students, and staff from outside China are drawn to NYU Shanghai by an interest in China. For their part, the students from China are attracted to an American university, studying alongside brilliant classmates from around the world, and circulating through the global network. As the first class prepared for graduation, they had been accepted to the finest graduate and professional schools in the world or received job offers at leading companies. Over 95 percent of the class was placed in graduate or professional schools or in a variety of professional and academic fields, including finance, law practice, interactive media arts, business management, and computer science.

The first decade of NYU's global network university has confirmed that the benefits of a university that encourages circulation among the world's idea capitals creates an irresistible draw for many of the smartest people in academe. Even those members of the NYU family who never leave New York (or Abu Dhabi, or Shanghai) reap the benefits of this model, as scholars who do circulate from other sites spend time with them, enhancing their academic life.

Criticisms of the Global Network University

Inevitably, given justifiable misgivings about the effects of economic globalization, serious commentators have raised questions about the NYU model. Four common critiques merit consideration: Is the global network university a form of intellectual imperialism? Is the global network university an inherently elitist concept? Can the highest academic standards be maintained in a global network university? And can a global network university be operated in a manner consistent with the core principles of a great liberal arts university?

CRITICISM 1: THE GLOBAL NETWORK CONSTITUTES INTELLECTUAL IMPERIALISM

The global network university at once is made possible by globalization and is a response to it. Yet globalization is controversial, generating not only hopes but also deep anxieties and resentments. The benefits of globalization are not evenly shared, and many fear that it is the latest form by which some areas of the world will dominate and exploit others.

The world, critics argue, has been "flattened" by globalization. And, the first steps toward the interconnected, globalized world so visible today came in the form of colonial expansion, political alliances, and trade relations. It is no surprise, then, that the first efforts to understand globalization—and to evaluate its tremendous impact on the lived reality of people around the world—have drawn heavily on politics and economics. In light of the historical background, commentators were quick to use analogies to colonization or franchising.

Such analogies are not, in my view, applicable in a discussion of the global network university. Education is not a commodity. The university's mission remains, even in an age when universities do behave like corporations in some areas of operation, the advancement of knowledge and the manifestation of the great rewards of learning. When universities "go global," their actions are (at least ideally) shaped by this mission, not by political or economic goals. And so long as a university remains true to these educational goals (this, of course, is a separate matter, which I will handle later), it is wrong to reduce its efforts to respond to globalization to politics and economics. Such reductionism ignores what universities can accomplish in the newly globalized world.

The experience of NYU at its Abu Dhabi and Shanghai portal campuses and its study-away sites is that the global network university is, in fact, an antidote to imperialism. Far from perpetuating old patterns of dominance and subordination, the global university offers opportunities for building through understanding a more just and elevated global civil society. As it broadens the opportunity for learning, this model of a university will bring greater equality of power. Rabbi Jonathan Sacks put it well in *The Dignity of Difference: How to Avoid the Clash of Civilizations*: "Education—the ability not merely to read and write but to master and apply information and have open access to knowledge—is essential to human dignity.

Because knowledge is power, equal access to knowledge is a precondition of equal access to power."[19]

The premise of the global network university is the idea that the most creative faculty, students, and administrators will be attracted to the opportunities for intellectual and cultural interchange that such a university provides. But critics argue that the process of selecting the few students from the many is elitist; they view this elitism as the perpetuation of dominance by those born to privilege.

True, the goal of the admissions process for the university I have described is to find "the best candidates"—in other words, an elite group. However, seeking an "elite" class based on merit is not elitism as long as: The norms of selection are fair, the university seeks those who are talented from all sectors of global society, and the university makes attendance possible financially and logistically.

The enormous effort NYU expends in finding and bringing to NYU Abu Dhabi and NYU Shanghai what is literally the most diverse group of students anywhere is especially notable. Each year, a team of admissions officers and nearly a thousand volunteer nominators work to identify talent where previously few had sought to find it. The students ultimately admitted come from every sector of society and from three-quarters of the nations in the world. They come from tribal villages and capital cities; they come from the higher, middle, and lower echelons of their societies; and nearly 20 percent of them had never been on a plane or left their home country before they boarded the flight that took them to the candidate interview weekend. And, when some of these talented students are admitted, the financial aid available guarantees that any worthy student can attend, thrive, and graduate debt free. The result of this extraordinary commitment is that meritorious young people who otherwise would not have the opportunity to study at a great university are able to do so. Simply put: This is a virtue.

CRITICISM 3: THE GLOBAL NETWORK WILL COMPROMISE ACADEMIC STANDARDS

What is common to all great universities—those with multiple locations in an organic circulatory network, those that combine a hub home campus with branch campuses, and those with a single traditional campus—is a commitment to academic excellence. A global network university, however, is still a novel notion; its fidelity to traditional academic standards is untested by time. Skeptics worry that this new form, spreading colleagues and classes across distant lands, will dilute academic standards.

Here again, NYU's experience is encouraging. A decade into its serious commitment to becoming a global network, NYU is much stronger academically than it would have been if it had stayed on a traditional path. World-class faculty, students, and staff have voted with their feet by joining the effort. Highly recruited graduate students, postdocs, and faculty now turn down offers from other prestigious universities to join teams at NYU's new campuses. Together they have created a research environment as strong as any in the world—with results that stand on a per capita basis with the very top universities in the world.

The undergraduate students are as good as any in the world, as measured by any standard. On every statistical measure, they are stronger than the classes admitted to NYU New York, which is itself highly selective. Overlap data, the measure of the choice made by students admitted to multiple schools, favors the two newest NYU campuses. Students who have a choice of attending either a traditional top-twenty school or either NYU Abu Dhabi or NYU Shanghai now usually choose to attend the NYU portal campus.

Faculty members, in Abu Dhabi, in Shanghai, and in New York (where students from Abu Dhabi and Shanghai often come to study away) consistently report that the students from Abu Dhabi or Shanghai stand with the very best students they have encountered. This sentiment is shared by faculty from other top universities who come to either of the new campuses for visiting semesters.

Far from diluting the quality of an NYU education and degree, NYU Abu Dhabi, NYU Shanghai, and the global network have elevated the quality of NYU. The New York campus is now far more selective by all criteria than it was a decade ago, with students citing the global network as a primary reason for their decision to choose NYU. Student retention has soared, as has graduates' satisfaction—again with students and alumni crediting the network as a main reason for their positive experience.

CRITICISM 4: THE GLOBAL NETWORK COMPROMISES CORE PRINCIPLES

Any great university is built upon the core values of intellectual integrity, a tolerance of difference, a willingness to examine and encourage unorthodox ideas, and an unflagging commitment to the pursuit of truth. A global network university must cherish and nurture these values. Skeptics say that it cannot.

By design, a global network university operates in many cultural contexts and in societies where the traditional core values of our universities are not honored as they are in America;

indeed, sometimes they are honored in the breach. To the extent that seeds of change are planted by the presence of universities that honor and advertise the benefits of these values, most would agree that there is movement in the right direction. That said, it is undeniable that those who are charged with building a university in such environments must take care to ensure that a virtuous effort to accommodate cultural differences does not compromise basic principles.

The perfect should not be allowed to drive out the good. If NYU refused to have a site in any city or country that did not meet fully its ideals, it would not be in New York City, let alone the United States. And, the same could be said about any of the other idea capitals in which the university has study-away sites. So, for example, during my time as NYU's president, an NYU law school professor who edited a scholarly journal was prosecuted under a French criminal statute for publishing a negative review of the work of a French scholar. Under the laws of the United Kingdom, public figures may bring defamation suits against those who criticize them without regard to the First Amendment protections of such criticism guaranteed in the American Constitution. Needless to say, NYU did not close its study-away sites in these two countries. Indeed, NYU opened its first study-away site in the Madrid of Spain's Generalissimo Francisco Franco, which was hardly a utopia.

None of the fourteen cities or countries in which NYU portal campuses or study-away sites are located is a perfect incarnation of the values of a great university. To make this point, one NYU Abu Dhabi student wrote a satirical magazine piece arguing for a boycott of NYU New York on the grounds that NYU should not be in a country where civil liberties were routinely violated. The question should not be: Does the local society meet that high standard? Rather it must be: Is it possible for the university to operate in this location with fidelity to the core principles that make universities great? Perhaps the most important of those principles are academic freedom and freedom of inquiry.

As of the time of this writing, NYU has had more than a decade of experience in Abu Dhabi and over five years of experience in Shanghai. Hundreds of faculty members have taught thousands of courses in the global network. Several hundred conferences, with speakers from around the world and across the ideological spectrum, have been convened in both settings on a wide range of topics. The experience of faculty, students, and others involved at the portal campuses and study-away sites unquestionably meets the norms of academic freedom and freedom of inquiry characteristic of NYU New York and its peer institutions. This assessment is shared by virtually all who have taught or studied on the campuses.

For example, I have taught my course, The Relationship of Government and Religion, in Abu Dhabi every year for over a decade and twice in Shanghai. I also teach it most years in New York. The subject matter—unedited Supreme Court opinions, including all dissents—is controversial in many ways. I use the same syllabus and readings in all three locations. I do not teach the course identically, but I have never modified the way I teach because of the site of my classroom.

When I begin each year, I tell the students that the primary purpose of the course is to teach them "a healthy disrespect for authority." I emphasize this not only to my NYU Abu Dhabi students in Abu Dhabi but also to the Emirati college students I teach there; and I always emphasize it to my NYU Shanghai students (once in a session attended by the Chinese minister of education). I always emphasize that the adjective *healthy* is meant to remind them that, when they question authority, they should have a reasoned explanation for doing so. I then urge them to begin by questioning my views and to observe the questioning of majority opinions by dissenting justices. It never has occurred to me that I should teach differently because I was in Abu Dhabi or Shanghai. Over the years, I have not experienced in either location any less freedom of discussion either in the exchanges in my classroom or in the conversations on campus. Colleagues on both campuses affirm that my experience is typical.

Academic freedom protects free inquiry and expression by those within the university, including both professors and students. However, *academic freedom* does not create unlimited *rights of expression* in every forum in every country where a campus is located. Academic freedom is a right that, by its nature, applies inside the university. As important as it is, academic freedom does not create in the professorate or academic class a set of uber-citizens who get superior rights of expression outside the walls of the university. The importance of the italicized words at the beginning of this paragraph is often lost in the heated conversations over this topic.

In the United States and around the world, the rights of expression beyond the university community are governed by the rules of the surrounding society. And the rules governing speech outside the university, on matters ranging from hate speech, to defamation, to pornography, to myriad other types of speech, differ in significant ways from jurisdiction to jurisdiction. In the United States, they often vary from state to state. A university has real power to insist on certain rules of expression within its walls—in other words, on academic freedom— but it does not have the right or the power (anywhere) to insist that the rules it adopts on campus be the rules of society. It can urge its view of the proper rule on society, but advocating a view, of course, is not the same as imposing it.

In Abu Dhabi, although the study of a work of art containing nudity would be acceptable in classroom discussion, it would be inappropriate to carry the work openly through the streets. Or, in Shanghai, although discussions in the classroom about a demonstration against the government would be fully protected by the academic freedom guaranteed on campus, any members of the NYU community who chose to participate in the demonstration would be subject to the law of China, with no special protection afforded if he or she wore an NYU sweatshirt. These examples illustrate a more general issue that universities face, whether they are global or traditional: necessary compliance with governing laws, even while seeking to change them. The issue is rarely one of academic freedom, although it is often articulated as if it were.

Some who have been critical of the global network university seem to believe that their academic status confers special rights of travel. In 2017, for example, two tenured professors who usually teach at NYU's New York campus asked to teach courses in Abu Dhabi. Their departments and the relevant deans in Abu Dhabi agreed; the respective courses were listed. One of the two, in fact, had taught at NYU Abu Dhabi twice before. However, when it came time for the professors to begin arranging their travel, Emirati authorities denied their necessary visas. One of the professors wrote an opinion piece in which he argued that the denial of visas showed that NYU Abu Dhabi's "promise of academic freedom has proved to be largely worthless."[20] He speculated that the reason for the denial was that he and the other professor were Shiites. He closed by urging that NYU acknowledge that "it has bought into a political system that actively discriminates against members of a religious minority because of an overwhelming fear of Iran and hatred of Shiites."[21] This claim, based on his speculation about the reason for the visa denials, was belied by the presence of the many Shiites already at NYU Abu Dhabi.

NYU and NYU Abu Dhabi long have stood against discrimination of any kind, including religious discrimination. In fact, one of my academic specialties is religious freedom. However, neither NYU nor any other university ever endorses the political system of any country in which it operates, including the United States.

When, a few weeks after the opinion piece appeared, I engaged one of these two colleagues (not the author of the article) in conversation, I asserted that there was no way that the university could guarantee unbridled movement across a sovereign border. He agreed. He also agreed that nobody at the university had promised such movement. Indeed, in an interesting coincidence, an NYU Abu Dhabi professor had been denied a visa to enter the United States around the same time. In the end, what my colleague wanted from the university was a vigorous statement of displeasure at the denial. Two days later, the university did issue such a statement, even as it continued to work more quietly with our Abu Dhabi government partners, as we do with the American government, to ensure that only legitimate security concerns are implicated whenever a visa is denied to an academic traveler.

In addition, the administration asked its standing Faculty Committee on the Global Network to look into general issues of mobility in the network and the specific issues raised by the denial of the two visas for the professors heading to Abu Dhabi. In its report, after initially noting that "NYUAD itself is a remarkable success story," the committee continued: "We have heard no evidence of obstacles to freedom in the classroom or in the area of research." It concluded: "As for global mobility, we are aware of no university in the world that can override a government's visa and security policies."[22]

NYU's experience with obtaining visas for faculty, students, and administrators in Abu Dhabi has been positive. In the first decade of activity there, 99 percent of requests for faculty visas and 99.9 percent of those for student visas were granted. The applicants came from 115 countries; included among them were Shia, Sunni, Christian, and Jewish believers. I understand the dismay of my two colleagues with the decisions on the visa applications they submitted. NYU publicly expressed its dissatisfaction. The government of the Emirates, like the government of the United States, does not explain such decisions. However, dissatisfaction with a visa decision comes nowhere near supporting a claim that the promise of academic freedom at NYU Abu Dhabi "is largely worthless."

There are other instances—still farther removed from the academic enterprise than the two I have just discussed, but nonetheless implicating values that are widely shared within the university community—where universities, global and traditional alike, operate in environments that tolerate conditions that are far less than ideal. NYU faculty, students, and staff in New York see homelessness and poverty every day that reminds them of this very sad reality.

One attack on NYU Abu Dhabi received considerable initial notoriety—although little coverage correcting the record after a comprehensive investigation proved the initial story misleading. The issue arose over the treatment of workers at NYU Abu Dhabi. Here is the story as I lived it.

NYU and those of us who crafted the original agreement with our Abu Dhabi partners have always advocated vigorously for workers' rights. As part of the memorandum setting the terms of the project, we included a set of labor standards that committed all contractors to treating workers well, throughout the creation of NYU Abu Dhabi. When the standards were made public, even Human Rights Watch (I say "even" because they had condemned the project before it began) praised them as a breakthrough and urged others to adopt what they saw as the platinum standards.

Fast-forward to May 2014. NYU Abu Dhabi was preparing for the graduation of the initial class of 140 young people from the first liberal arts college created by an American research university in the Gulf. The class featured three Rhodes Scholars, including an Emirati woman. President Bill Clinton delivered the first commencement address. Against that background, an article appeared on the front page of the *New York Times* bearing the headline: "Workers at NYU's Abu Dhabi Site Faced Harsh Conditions."[23] This article, which time and investigation would show to be a misrepresentation of the reality on the ground, dominated the news about NYU Abu Dhabi that week, overshadowing the extraordinary achievement celebrated six days later at the graduation ceremony. To this day, many cite the article as if it has not been debunked. I will devote attention to it here to set the record straight.

The opening four paragraphs of the piece recounted an incident in which striking workers in the Emirates, allegedly working for NYU, were beaten and then deported for illegal activities. It went on, with several accompanying pictures, to report that "some men lived in squalor, 15 men to a room." The article noted that the UK engineering firm that had been hired by NYU and its partners to monitor compliance, interviewing workers regularly, had reported that "overall, there is strong evidence confirming the NYUAD project is taking workers' rights seriously." But, the article went on to say, the monitor had made "no mention of the strike or the strikers' demands for more pay," and it failed to note the NYU spokesman's claim "that university officials were not aware of any unrest." Apparently, the doubly asserted lack of awareness, coming from both the monitor and NYU officials, raised no warning flags for the reporter that the treatment described might not have involved NYU. For their part, the university and its government partners reaffirmed commitment to the labor standards and apologized for whatever violations *might* have occurred. They pledged an independent investigation, the results to be reported transparently.

The independent investigation, conducted by a former U.S. attorney and a large team he assembled, took nearly a year, involved hundreds of interviews, spanned several countries, and culminated in a public report of 72 pages. Acknowledging, as even the original *New York Times* article had, that NYU and its government partners had accepted a considerable challenge by articulating the labor standards involved, the report confirmed that NYU and its partners made good-faith efforts to implement and enforce the standards fully. These efforts benefited the substantial majority of the approximately thirty thousand individuals who worked on the construction of the campus. The report also found that the labor-compliance monitoring program effectively and routinely identified and resolved issues of contractor noncompliance.[24]

There was, however, an important gap in the system, which adversely affected a subset of workers. Unbeknownst to either NYU or its Abu Dhabi partners, the British general contractor had exempted inappropriately from the labor standards small and short-term subcontractors (those with contracts below a million dollars or fewer than thirty days on the project). Up to a third of those who had worked on the site potentially could have been affected by this error. In response to this finding, the university and its Abu Dhabi partners commissioned an outside expert to locate and compensate any workers who had not received the treatment and entitlements promised in the labor standards. This process, which took over a year, did eventually reach and reimburse the great majority of the workers.

The report's most illuminating finding was that the genesis of the strike at the emotional center of the article was not as the article had portrayed it. The *Times* article had suggested that worker dissatisfaction with low wages at the NYU site was the cause of the strike. In fact, the strike was not in any respect a protest of treatment at the NYU site—quite the opposite. Some of the striking workers had indeed done work on the NYU site, but they had moved on to other sites well before the strike. What the strikers wanted was that their later employer adopt better conditions—comparable to those at NYUAD. This finding turns the conclusion of the misreported *Times* article on its head. The true story of the strike was not one of poor conditions at the NYU site, but of how the NYUAD project set high standards that the workers sought to generalize.

Then there were the images. The article states that the workers were housed by their employer-subcontractor, City Falcon, "in a small tenement building in the city's tenement district." City Falcon, indeed, did have a very small sub-subcontract on the NYUAD site, involving around nine workers for a period of four months. Their contract was improperly exempted from compliance with the labor standards and they were owed wages. That said, the front-page photo represented was not of the housing conditions for workers on the NYU project. The article later calls into question the quality of the housing for the "vast majority of the roughly 6,000 [sic] people" who built the campus, but the actual accommodations (for the nearer to thirty thousand who worked on the project) were nothing like the photos. The housing provided for the NYU project was new, clean, and met or exceeded U.S. Occupational Safety and Health Administration standards for such facilities. It provided cafeterias, cricket pitches, other recreational facilities, and computers with internet access. As the investigator's report stated, workers "gave positive reviews of the living conditions [in these facilities], with many stating that the conditions were superior to those at other accommodations where they had previously resided."

I will summarize the rest of this saga with the story of just one meeting.

It took place in my office in the summer of 2015. Present, in addition to me, were NYU's provost, executive vice president, and chief press officer, the executive director of Human Rights Watch (HRW), the director of HRW's Middle East / North Africa region, and a senior board member of HRW. The meeting had been called because, although HRW initially had been very critical of the NYU project, the board member thought there was a possibility that HRW would acknowledge publicly the fact that NYU and its partners had done a great deal to raise the conditions of workers both directly through its projects and indirectly by offering a standard that others could be called to meet.

There was consensus in the room on several major accomplishments, in addition to the enactment of the labor standards themselves. First, the standards had been very well implemented in all the operations, from maintenance to security to cleaning to transportation, under the direct supervision of NYU Abu Dhabi and its Abu Dhabi partners. Second, the safety record at the construction site was truly exceptional. Third, the labor standards indisputably raised the conditions substantially of nearly 70 percent of the workers on the new campus construction site at the time of their employment. And fourth, when presented by the independent fact-finder with evidence that some sub-contractors had been improperly exempted from the standards, the university and its partners had gone to great lengths to ensure the workers received the compensation to which they were entitled.

I summarized the consensus as I heard it: NYU and its government partners had taken a very difficult exam and had earned a grade of A–, which should be celebrated. The conditions and lives of the workers had been advanced materially. And it would be unfair and misleading, as had been the case, to publish only the "wrong answers" on the exam. The HRW board member and executive director agreed, and the executive director pledged to call public attention to these accomplishments. It has been three years since the meeting; yet, there has been no statement from HRW or its executive director acknowledging the achievements we listed that morning.

While such silence is unfortunate, I don't doubt that many of our critics are motivated by a sincere interest in improving the conditions of migrant workers. What I do know is that NYU and its Abu Dhabi partners share this motivation entirely. And I believe that a full assessment of labor compliance at NYU Abu Dhabi shows that, despite some shortcomings and lessons learned, the project tangibly improved workers' lives. As the investigative report stated, "Many workers described their employment on the [NYU] Campus Project in favorable terms, with a number saying it was the best project they had ever worked on."[25]

The construction of the campus was completed years ago; there no longer are tens of thousands of workers on a massive building project. And, the treatment of workers on campus who have been employed directly by NYU, or by contractors supervised by NYU and its partners, never has been an issue— a positive record has been sustained in the intervening years. The university and its partners have established an ongoing compliance program that includes an in-house, on-the-ground team who routinely interview workers and audit employer compliance with the labor standards, as well as a 24/7 hotline that anyone can call to report a compliance concern.

The effectiveness of these measures is in turn monitored by an internationally recognized, independent labor-compliance monitor, Impact Ltd. After its review of activity between December 2015 and March 2018, it "identified a good level of compliance among contractors and a high level of satisfaction among workers." And, based upon interviews with more than five hundred workers, it also found that "these positive results correlate with anecdotal worker accounts from audit interviews, where workers reported on numerous occasions positive experiences working on the NYUAD project, compared to other projects or jobs."[26]

The Criticisms in Perspective

Any college or university leader who attempts to move a traditional university in the direction of a global university is very likely to encounter the kinds of arguments I have just discussed. Criticism about academic quality and core values implicates threshold issues that a university leader must resolve satisfactorily with the potential hosts and partners before a move forward is undertaken. Other criticisms—those born of stereotypes or ignorance of other peoples—underscore the case for moving ahead. But perfection cannot be the standard, for no university anywhere is perfect. Criticism must be placed in context, specifically the context of the good that is accomplished by the project for the university, its constituents, the host community, and the world.

In 2015, a spectacularly brilliant Emirati woman, a graduate of Harvard College and Columbia Law School who forswore an advancing legal career in one of New York's top law firms to return home to be the chairman of NYU Abu Dhabi's governmental partner, received the first Vice Chancellor's Medal conferred by NYU on the Abu Dhabi campus. In an eloquent acceptance address, she summarized the NYU Abu Dhabi initiative:

> As I look around me today, I am overwhelmed. It is one thing for us to dream. But it is entirely different to see the dream come to life—to see all of you grow and create a community that is richer than we could have dreamed.
>
> We sought to create a new way to learn and to educate, not just for us in Abu Dhabi, but also as a contribution to the global community.
>
> Our wish was for a place where people could: encounter a foreign idea or a foreign person without fear or the desire to marginalize; value each other and search for commonalities and goodness as a first instinct; and, in those cases where agreement is not possible, disagree in a constructive and respectful way.
>
> We wanted to create a special environment, a forum for engagement and understanding among people of many different perspectives. The things that united us would be: understanding, dialogue, openness, tolerance, public service, mutual respect, and (perhaps more importantly) mutual responsibility. Quite a tall order.[27]

There will be challenges in the coming years, in Abu Dhabi and Shanghai, as in every other NYU site—including Greenwich Village. The challenges will be a test of the NYU leadership as much as of our hosts, a test of our capacity to avoid ethnocentricity and cultural chauvinism, of our ability to act in ways that recognize that we are in a different cultural context. The portal campuses of the global network university were established in Abu Dhabi and Shanghai rather than in Philadelphia or Toronto so as to take faculty, students, and staff out of their comfort zones and provoke the development of the cultural competence that is an essential dialogic skill in the Second Axial Age. Being at any site is not the same as being in New York, which is why we are there. In Abu Dhabi, or in Shanghai, we do not want to be an exact replica of the university we are in New York; rather, we want to be a version of ourselves of which we can be proud and which is appropriate for the context. There are and will be growing pains; but, so long as they are addressed with fidelity to the core of a great university, the global network university—the ecumenical university—will help shape a hopeful future.

Living in the Global Network University

For more than a decade, I have lived a version of NYU's network. I know the stories of scores of its faculty and staff, and the tales of thousands of students. There is something indescribable and beyond words about life in the global network university. Rarely in my life have friends and associates accused me of understatement, but dozens of them, after glimpsing the reality of daily life in the university that is now NYU, have said that this new version of what a university could be is far better than anything they had been led by my statements to believe. Let me nonetheless try, in the next few pages, to describe to you how those of us who are involved feel about our day-to-day experience of it.

NYU now is a union of three distinct university personalities: New York, Abu Dhabi, and Shanghai.

The New York campus is massive, nearly sixty thousand students, spread across two dozen schools, with thousands of full-time faculty members and additional thousands of part-time faculty. In a way that mirrors New York City, NYU embodies the challenges and the rewards of complexity, within the university as well as in the city. The university is aggressive in putting a safety net of wellness programs in place, but it does so to encourage students to go beyond their natural comfort zones, knowing the safety net is there to help.

From their very first contact with the university, faculty and students are told that finding community at NYU New York will require effort. NYU New York is a university without a campus, in and of the world's most heterogeneous city. The deliberate strategy of NYU New York is to seize that complexity as a learning opportunity, a way to hone ecumenical skills.

The student body at NYU New York has a healthy representation of students from outside the United States. In the most recent undergraduate class, just under 25 percent of freshmen carried foreign passports—even though there was no targeted effort to attract foreign students. There is an even larger percentage of foreign students in graduate schools and professional school programs. Still, with 75 percent of its students coming from America, NYU New York has a predominantly American ethos. And New York, although the incarnation of ecumenism, is an American city. The Americans who have chosen NYU New York are either native New Yorkers or those who want to live or study in New York; they are cosmopolitans, but they are American cosmopolitans.

NYU Abu Dhabi is 180 degrees different from NYU New York. When it is fully grown, it will house about sixteen hundred undergraduates and up to five hundred graduate students and postdocs. Already, with about twelve hundred undergraduates, over one hundred fifteen countries are represented in the student body, with students from the UAE comprising the largest group (at about 15 percent) and students from the United States the next largest contingent (at about 14 percent). With such a small population, faculty and students form a community without much effort. The unique feature of the community is its concentrated diversity; no other student body in the world is so intensely diverse.

So if a faculty member or student chooses NYU Abu Dhabi, he or she will encounter highly concentrated complexity in a community that is a microcosm of the world. To thrive, he or she must embrace regular, close encounters with those who are different—and rejoice in them. On campus, all of humanity is in your life every day. And so it is on the streets of Abu Dhabi, a city where about 15 percent of the residents are citizens of the UAE, and where the other residents are citizens of over two hundred countries.

The NYU Shanghai community—50 percent Chinese and 50 percent from outside of China—is only a little larger than NYU Abu Dhabi. So, if a faculty member or student chooses Shanghai, he or she, like an NYU Abu Dhabi counterpart, will find the same concentrated complexity and diversity in a community, but with a powerful Chinese presence. This signature characteristic is evident on day one, when each Chinese student is assigned a roommate from outside China, and it continues as a theme on campus. All students must be fluent in Chinese to graduate. And, of course, Shanghai arguably is China's most global city.

A feature of life in NYU's global network university is that neither faculty members nor students are confined to the portal campus that serves as their point of entry. In the three weeks of January terms or in semesters away, faculty and students of all three sites mingle formally and informally with each other. It follows that even a person who chooses the experience of a single campus will benefit from exposure to others from the network.

From the early days of the global network, I have been an active participant in its wonders. I taught in Abu Dhabi from the very beginning—and every year since. By 2015, I was teaching four different versions of my course, in all three locations.

Trust me: Working with these four sets of students simultaneously has been the most rewarding teaching experience of my six decades in the classroom. And, by the way, I *am* in the classroom, not on a computer or a screen. When my friends ask how I weather the peripatetic nature of my travel schedule as I move among these cities, I tell them it is energizing. To work in class with some of the world's brightest young people, to watch their minds open to new ways of thinking, to follow them as they come to love material I love, and to see familiar material through their fresh eyes: These are the special joys of a teaching life.

Over the decades, I have taught students who went on to be presidents of some of the nation's top colleges, deans of leading law schools, judges on some of our highest courts, internationally honored scholars, and others who have been major forces in myriad areas. I am generally considered a very effective teacher. Yet, in the fall of 2008, a few days before my first class in Abu Dhabi with the twenty inaugural students in the local scholars' program (all Emirati and all Muslim), I was very, very worried about how I would do. And my worry was orders of magnitude greater than the usual anxiety any good teacher feels as a new semester begins.

Before I met them and worked with them on the material, I worried that they might well not accept my basic premise—that they could advance their knowledge through critical thinking. I recalled my own view at their age: that the real truths were not to be discovered through reason but through revelation (for me, curated by the pope and the Church). As I flew to my first class in Abu Dhabi filled with all of the stereotypes Americans are taught about the region, I worried that the twenty young people I would meet might be where I was then—that they would dismiss my effort to develop in them the skills of critical reasoning and argumentation as a misguided attempt to undermine a truth they knew.

I am embarrassed that I was not prepared for what became one of my most exhilarating classroom experiences, testimony to Charlie's great wisdom in seeing the joy of playing new octaves. Over the next eight months, I went on a magical intellectual journey with those seventeen women and three men as we parsed the reasoning of the majority and dissenting opinions in dozens of major Supreme Court cases. As one student put it in two of the twelve stanzas of a poem she wrote as a gift to me at the end of the year:

> Because all good things must come to an end,
> When we say farewell
> After all these months of pretending to be lawyers and Justices,
> Picking on each other, only to laugh about it later,
> Slapping each other's backs for an argument well fought.
>
> Because all good things must come to an end,
> When we say farewell
> After all these months of drawing a crooked line in the sand between right and wrong,
> Deciding what is permissible and what is not,
> And then erasing it, only to draw another.

I framed that poem, written in her beautiful script on parchment. It now hangs on the wall just outside my New York office door as a reminder of that wonderful class and the vigor they brought to mastering exegesis and critical thinking.

As special as that first class of Emirati scholars was, the scholars who followed were just as distinctive. Every year, I have looked forward to my meetings with these citizens of a world I could not have imagined when I was their age. Typical is the annual discussion of a case I always assign, the Supreme Court's opinion in *Board of Education v. Allen* (1968).

At stake in *Allen* was the constitutionality, under the doctrine of separation of church and state, of a New York statute that authorized authorities to provide free textbooks to children attending private schools, including religious ones. The Court (by a 6–3 vote) accepted the validity of the statute. Justice Douglas, writing in dissent, argued strenuously that a textbook was not a "neutral" item—because how it was used depended very much on who the teacher was. He wrote: "The Crusades, for example, may be taught as a Christian undertaking to 'save the Holy Land' from the Moslem Turks who 'became a threat to Christianity and its holy places' which 'they did not treat with respect,' or as essentially a series of wars born out of political and materialistic motives."[28]

In every one of the twelve classes I have taught to my Emirati students, they have initiated a conversation about how apparently objective tools, such as maps, might consciously or unconsciously be used by a teacher to shape conclusions. And in every one of those classes, on their own, they have begun to reexamine their own education through this critical lens.

Just as these students traveled to intellectual places that were new to them, so also the students who come to NYU Abu Dhabi literally experience a place that, but for NYU Abu

Dhabi, would not have been part of their lives. To teach such students, who are every bit as brilliant and dedicated to their classwork as they are diverse in background, is a great honor—and another experience I never could have imagined a few years ago. But there is one feature of the NYU Abu Dhabi class among all others that makes teaching there even more special than a casual observer might realize: A healthy percentage of each entering class might not have been discovered at all were it not for the school's aggressive search for talent in places where most of the world's top schools never look.

In my first NYU Abu Dhabi class, there was a young man who had taught himself in a tribal village in Ethiopia. After doing the first eight grades on his own, he (then thirteen years old) walked five days by himself to Addis Ababa, where he gained admission to the international school. (The school gave him a scholarship and, after discovering he was living in the airport, supplemented it with room and board.) After he graduated at the top of the class, we brought him to NYU Abu Dhabi.

This story is dramatic but not unusual at NYU Abu Dhabi. Whether it is a young man who survived, with one sibling, the slaughter of his parents and nine siblings in the Rwandan genocide, or the young woman from rural Afghanistan, or the homeless Russian orphan who taught himself on the streets, or the son of a rural West Virginia single mother, the stories of a substantial percentage of the NYU Abu Dhabi students are astonishing and inspiring. When they bring their experiences—and their love of learning—to class, they enrich the conversation, elevate the preparedness of the entire class (because nobody slacks off in the presence of classmates who value education as these students do), and create for the professor a joy in teaching that is beyond words.

Lastly, the final piece of the puzzle falls into place: NYU Shanghai. Here again, the student body is exceptional and unlike any other in the world, with the sole exception of NYU Abu Dhabi's. And, as in Abu Dhabi, there are moving stories to tell about the students—for example, the story of one young Ohio woman who had not been out of her state until she got on the plane to Shanghai.

My course, which requires about two hundred pages of reading plus a written paper for each class, is quite demanding for those for whom English is a second, third, or even fourth language. Most years, my Abu Dhabi class meets every two weeks for the entire school year, but in Shanghai it meets every week for one semester. This pace is not an issue for the American students or for those from English-fluent countries. But for the half of the class that is Chinese, it is a real challenge. Still, they revel in the challenge and uniformly encourage me not to let the course become "thinner." Their capacities grow, discernibly and rapidly—and they inspire me and their classmates to put even more effort into each class.

What most differentiates the classroom discussion in Shanghai is the fact that about 80 percent of the Chinese students have no concept of what religion is. Since the course is on the relationship of government and religion, religion is a key referent. To teach the course to students, some of whom have no concept of why religious adherents (let alone a religious martyr) would care so much, is mind-twistingly wonderful.

There is a tradition about the final class of my course that has survived the journey across cultural and geographic boundaries: the Steel Cage Match. For this class, students read a 1978 article in the *Harvard Law Review* that offers a definition of the word *religion* in the First Amendment to the American Constitution. I wrote the piece. The class consists of a debate between each of the students and me, each of them in turn attacking the piece in an eight-minute exchange, after which a panel of seven judges (faculty and former students) individually raise ballots declaring who won the debate, the student or me. For each ballot the student earns, he or she gets an extra lottery ticket in a raffle held at the end of class. Four tickets are drawn and the winners are rewarded with an outing (for example, a day of paragliding with me).

When graduates return to observe the class in later years, as they frequently do, they often offer the Steel Cage Match as their most vivid memory. There is no doubt that, in their preparation for that class, students do some of their closest analysis of cases and text. They certainly do some of their most rigorous thinking as they prepare their arguments. And in hours of mock debates with each other, they learn oral advocacy and teamwork. But there is one overriding lesson: a healthy questioning of authority. For a young Emirati woman, or a young Chinese man, or a young man from an Ethiopian refugee camp, or a young American dreamer to stand toe-to-toe with a professor in a debate where they are attacking his work—for that to happen is magic! A teacher's dream.

I started this chapter by listing the peripatetic travel schedule of my teaching life. I hope these stories give a sense of why I find such travel fulfilling. The teaching life may not be everyone's calling, but for those who are summoned to this life, it does not get any better than what I have.

Sustaining the Global University: Toward and Beyond 2050

Given the state of the United States and the world today, many find it hard each morning to approach the day with hope. There are powerful forces at work to dismantle the structure of global cooperation and interconnectivity that enlightened leaders worked to build over the seven decades since World War II. With the current wave of nativism, and with anxiety about borders and boundaries, some argue that now is the worst of times for a global network university.

My answer is that there has never been a time when the creation of such a university is more important. Now we can see an institution that incarnates cooperation and interconnectivity: the global network university and its citizens, a growing cohort of cosmopolitans committed to spreading its values. The question now is whether such a university is sustainable.

At present, NYU is the first and most highly developed version of this form of university. And there is every indication that the new NYU leadership will stay the course. However, even if NYU were to abandon the effort, there will be others. In that sense, the particular direction undertaken by NYU is not relevant in answering the question of ultimate sustainability. On the other hand, the indisputable success so far of NYU is what draws the attention of others who may attempt to adopt the model or a version of it: How the future unfolds at NYU will be relevant to the willingness of others to go forward. So, I will focus my attention on what I see ahead for NYU.

This question of sustainability is not about next year, or even a decade from now. The short term is not the issue. NYU's global network university, like all universities, will be measured in generations. The seeds have been planted, and, for more than a decade, the plants have been nurtured into saplings. And collectively—not unanimously, but collectively—the faculty members at NYU, especially those who have experienced the network, have embraced the notion of the global network as a defining element of NYU. There is a natural momentum now: Faculty and students come to NYU for the experience that the global university uniquely provides, which creates a reinforcing virtuous circle of talent that bodes well.

So what are the new challenges that are ahead, external and internal?

It is possible that geopolitical changes might affect the viability of one or more of the portal campuses. China and the Gulf, for example, are epicenters of tectonic change, not all of which is certain to play out in ways favorable to the global network. Presently, we can make the case that the presence of the university creates momentum in a positive direction. But there are no guarantees for the future. The university must be vigilant, always placing above all else the safety of faculty, students, and staff.

It also is possible that the university's extraordinary partners in Abu Dhabi or Shanghai might become less willing to provide crucial financial support. To date, there is no hint of that. In Abu Dhabi, investment in NYU Abu Dhabi remained a top priority even as the Emirate absorbed the effects of the 2009 financial crisis and a dramatic decline in the price of oil. Its commitment to building academic and research excellence on campus remained the guiding principle of the project. If anything, given the success of the effort so far, there is powerful evidence of greater commitment by NYU's Abu Dhabi partners. A five-year review by NYU's partners in Shanghai has led to plans for expanding the effort there. For the foreseeable future, the commitment of NYU's partners is solid.

However, although I do not worry very much about the possible external factors that might slow the development of the global network university, I do worry a bit about internal factors that might compromise what can be accomplished by the NYU experiment. These internal factors do not so much pose a threat to the success of NYU Abu Dhabi, NYU Shanghai, or the global network, but they may limit the scope of the potential transformation of higher education.

The faculty and students are adventurous and cosmopolitan. Yet the faculty, who are the principal stewards of the enterprise because of their long-standing involvement in it, were raised, ratified, and deemed exceptional by the *traditional* standards of academic excellence. Although they later came to embrace the more expansive standards of the global university, their internalization of more traditional standards exerts a powerful pull toward reversion to those modes of activity. This natural—even virtuous—behavior will not compromise excellence as assessed by the old norms, but it likely will limit the potential impact of the global network university. This, in my view, would be lamentable.

A few examples will illustrate how a process of reversion to the old ways might occur inadvertently if the stewards of the university do not take care to reaffirm the essential theory of the enterprise, ensuring that whatever change occurs is a consequence of deliberate choice.

The NYU Abu Dhabi standing faculty (those who spend more than 80 percent of their time at the Abu Dhabi campus) now exceeds two hundred, across departments in every discipline. This cohort is complemented by four hundred postdocs, research fellows, graduate assistants, and instructors also in full-time residence. Since NYU Shanghai started three years after Abu Dhabi, the standing faculty and complementary academic team are smaller there but growing to similar levels. On both campuses, these academics are joined by affiliated faculty from NYU New York who come, typically, for a semester or a year, although after an interval many return for future terms.

As the standing faculties grow on each campus, they or others in authority might well be attracted to a number of policy changes, all potentially compromising the circulatory nature of the global network. Each change could be justified on the logic, long used to confine faculty and students to local campuses, that the (now substantial) local faculty knows and implements best the "special approach" of the campus it has created and best understands and embodies its values. By this logic, the faculty might urge a greater number of local appointments and fewer invitations to affiliated faculty from New York to teach; or, the faculty might place restrictions on the study-away opportunities (semesters and January terms) offered to students. Gradually an ethos of autonomy rather than connectivity would emerge to supplant the circulatory nature that provides unique strengths to the global university. The movement among idea capitals would diminish and the circulatory system would become sclerotic.

Students live campus life in cyclical, rather than linear, time. Their sense of the enterprise begins with their arrival. Absent intervention by agents, faculty and otherwise, to tell the story (the mythos) of the university, freshmen believe that the university they encounter as they arrive is the university that always has been. Since the reversion to traditional modalities, if it occurs, will take place slowly over time, new faculty and students are unlikely to provide a check on the movement away from some of the innovative early practices, unless the active involvement of those who preceded them provides institutional memory.

For this and other reasons, the graduates of the global network university—and especially those of NYU Abu Dhabi and NYU Shanghai—have a critical role to play in sustaining the unique elements of the enterprise. They are not traditional alumni, to be informed of the latest campus news and brought to campus periodically for nostalgic reunions. Rather, they are an important component of the institutional memory, stewards of the mission. Further, they are a good network of ambassadors for the ecumenical view of the world, spread out around the globe, but connected in a common effort to advance each other's lot and to promote the values inculcated in them through this education. Building the network of the graduates and connecting them to students on campus is not the traditional role of a university's alumni office. But to maximize the impact of the global university, this network must be built.

For NYU, the move to becoming a global network was natural. Its location in the world's capital city meant that its faculty and students already embraced the core concept—a secular ecumenism—of the global network university. And, from its founding, NYU has had a history of innovation; it has been called "the finest university that will try something that has a real chance of failing."

There are other fine universities, which are more risk averse, that have prided themselves on shaping their nation's leaders and increasingly on having a role in global society. As the NYU experiment continues to succeed, these leading universities, especially those blessed with huge financial assets, will create alternative versions of the global model.

In the end, the success of the global network model does not depend on the success of its first instantiation; but, to return to where we began, our capacity to move to the ecumenical world may well depend on whether at least a few universities move beyond traditional notions of what a university is to embrace some version of this new model.

4

The Final Ingredient
Meaningful Access for All

Prelude

My argument has come to this point: There is an exigent need to replace the rampant secular dogmatism that infects society. Traditional universities have a capacity and a duty to act as an antidote to this social disease. Beyond this, there are some universities—the global ones—that self-consciously should serve as incubators for a new secular ecumenism. This effort will not succeed, however, unless we ensure that all whose talents and passions warrant a seat in a college or university are able to obtain that seat—and with it, the education to which they are entitled and a voice in the ecumenical conversation. We are far from that goal.

Today, terrible disparities of wealth and opportunity—in the United States and, still more gravely, in the wider world—leave children without the education they deserve. As a result, millions never fully realize the lives they might have lived, humankind never benefits from their talent, and important perspectives are marginalized. In short, everyone loses.

It would be ironic if, in the process of creating universities designed to foster secular ecumenism, we excluded whole communities. If we hope to create an ecumenical world, every citizen of that world must have the opportunity to acquire the tools that can be used to enrich their own lives, to advance understanding, and to participate in shaping our collective future. All those who have the talent and the will, wherever they are, must be part of the project.

Too many people—from pundits to politicians to philanthropists—are promoting policies that undermine the quality of what our colleges and universities do and that, intentionally or not, restrict meaningful access for talented young people born in the wrong zip code or in the wrong region of the world. There is a possibility that education (and particularly higher education), long the great instrument of upward mobility, will become a tool of social stratification. Leaders who avidly seek seats for their own children in the most expensive schools and colleges—from $40,000 kindergartens to $60,000 colleges—rest easy, having (unintentionally, I hope) relegated the children of the poor, the middle class, the uninformed, and the unconnected to colleges or universities to which they never would send their own progeny. If this situation continues, the resulting division will exacerbate what President Obama called "the nagging feeling" among those who are excluded that "the deck is stacked against them," and that feeling in turn will fuel the growth of distrust in society. This alienation is inimical to the creation of the world we seek.

In the pages that follow, I focus primarily on higher-education policy in America, although what I will say about the state of higher education in my country applies with even greater force to most other parts of the world. Although the disparities I observe in higher education are mirrored in primary and secondary education, my argument is that meaningful access for all is a sine qua non of the ecumenical university.

The Status Quo: Excellence for a Few

Even in these times of austerity, most of our leaders at least pay lip service to the proposition that we must find a way to achieve excellence in the education we offer our citizens. Yet many who shape our policies and many in the commentariat do not support the investment that is its predicate. Instead, they offer unsupported claims that the cost of higher education can be reduced significantly without compromising quality—a false proposition that, in my view, may well have disastrous results.

The time has come for a conversation about how we might provide meaningful access to the education that maximizes the individual potential of each person who can benefit from what our colleges and universities offer. And it must be an informed conversation, one that moves beyond facile catch phrases and headlines. The quality of our future depends on it.

The best of American colleges and universities are, for the moment, the world standard. As problematic as rankings are, it is noteworthy that for many years and across various measures American universities have dominated the lists. In virtually every survey, America's universities occupy two-thirds or more of the top ten spots; the percentage holds among the top fifty or top hundred.[1] Moreover, each year the strength of American colleges and universities is reaffirmed by their capacity to attract talented scholars, teachers, and international students in numbers far exceeding any other country's.

Of course, not all American colleges and universities are excellent. Some are mediocre or downright bad. This is particularly true in the for-profit sector where the education is often very poor, completion rates are scandalously low, and students can be left with debt but without the degree for which it was incurred. But, mediocrity is not limited to the for-profit sector; there are also not-for-profit or state-run schools that perform badly.

I will not defend colleges and universities that are not providing value. And I believe that higher-education policy must be structured to penalize those institutions that are not performing and reward those that are. I applaud performance-based funding, as long as the criteria are carefully constructed. We should do everything possible to eliminate those schools that are not meeting standards. Their deficient performance should not be allowed to hide behind excellence elsewhere in the system. Yet, even if every low-performing college and university were closed, we would have done little to address the most serious problem facing higher education.

Around the globe, policy makers are discussing the "massification" of education—how society can bring education (and, ultimately, higher education) to the world's billions. The American version of this conversation is about access and attainment. But focusing simply on the number who enter school, remain in school, and attain degrees is a mistake unless the degrees are high-quality degrees and suited to the students who obtain them. My fear is that the conversations about massification are part of a reductive trend toward simplistic, quantifiable, and easily achievable goals. This trend, in turn, will exaggerate a stratification of education—with only the well-informed and the well-resourced receiving the highest-quality education, and with students who could thrive and blossom, if given the chance, relegated instead to a larger "common" pool, their talents underdeveloped or lost.

Not every student—not even every high school graduate—should pursue a college degree. People are different, and so are their capacities, passions, and interests. Some do not have the intellectual capacity to do college work; others lack the desire or the discipline to do the work; still others have a passion that takes them in a direction that requires different training. It serves no purpose to entice everyone into college, and it is subversive to dilute the content of college degrees so that the recipients of that degree can be counted as graduates in a politically inspired statistical contest. But, we must ensure that those students who do go to college attend schools that match their talents and needs. In other words, we must provide them *meaningful* access.

The conversation about higher education often is infected with what I call the fungibility fallacy. Most of us understand that homes, cars, or vacations are not all the same, and that variations in price generally reflect differences in quality. Yet much of the discussion about higher education proceeds as if all degrees were the same. This is a dangerous way to frame the conversation.

If the conversation continues to be framed in this way, we run the risk that the easiest way for political leaders to achieve the goals they set on access and attainment ("massification") will be to settle for the least expensive and most easily administered option for most students (excepting, of course, students from their own families), hollowing out the content and meaning of the degrees obtained. If all degrees are equal, this stance becomes palatable and defensible in the public square. The resulting statistics will show increases in enrollment and graduation rates, but the progress will be a sham.

As is often the case, the easiest way is not the wisest way. Although we cannot afford to lose a single mind, there is strong evidence that the children of those who are less informed and less resourced tend to choose schools that have less to offer them over schools chosen by similarly qualified children of parents who are better connected, informed, and resourced. The real challenge is to match each student with the option most appropriate for him or her within our remarkably diverse higher-education system and to see them through to a completed degree that is worthy of them.

There are millions of Americans, and many millions more elsewhere, who should go to college but do not. This situation is lamentable, since the lives of these students could be greatly enhanced by a match between them and the right school—a goal that could be accomplished using tools that are already available. This is not a disease for which a cure must be discovered. We know the answers: information, guidance, motivation, and resources.

Matching Students with the Right Educational Pathway

Over 150 years ago, John Cardinal Newman outlined his "idea of a university." According to Newman, a university education should entail the pursuit of knowledge for its own sake; feature a mentoring relationship between professors and students; cultivate the ways of the mind and critical thinking, with little regard for vocational preparation; and build character.[2]

Years later, Jaroslav Pelikan, in homage to Newman, described the university Newman would have created if he had known of the modern research university. It was a university that placed the elements of the education Newman had envisioned in the context of research on the frontiers of knowledge, integrating even undergraduates into the processes of idea creation through meaningful contact with those doing the research.[3] This dimension was a significant addition to Newman's ideal, but, magnificent as it is, it adds only one element to the increasingly complex picture of higher education.

The structure developed in the 1950s by Clark Kerr for the University of California system provides a starting point for understanding this complexity. Kerr's plan was a three-tier system. Research universities provide undergraduate, graduate, and professional education and are the locus of research activity, which itself provides a context, formal and informal, for all levels of instruction. The comprehensive universities focus on under-graduate education, even as they offer some graduate education. The community colleges offer academic and vocational instruc-tion to students through the first two years of an undergraduate education (culminating in associate degrees), and provide work-force training courses (culminating in certificates).

Today, we supplement Kerr's three-part structure with both technical colleges (for example, in engineering) and spe-cialty colleges (for example, in the performing arts), each of which might offer programs from the most basic to the most advanced, featuring research as well as instruction.

Then we add private universities—some with one of the structures just described; some with differentiating elements, such as NYU's focus on preparing students to lead a globalized world. Others, such as the faith-based colleges and universities, focus on moral development in a particular tradition.

Finally, there are the various possibilities created by the introduction of technology, both as an independent medium (with full degrees offered online) and as an element of each of the various models already listed. McKinsey reports that more than 30 percent of American college and university students are already taking at least one course for credit online.[4] Whether it is supporting independent programs or adding another element to existing ones, technology is an important feature of the emerging higher-education landscape.

This quick review of the evolution of higher education over a century reveals its extraordinary diversity. The American system is comprised of over four thousand institutions, large and small, urban and rural, public and private, faith-based and secular. They range from research universities to classic liberal arts colleges, to technical colleges, to community colleges; and their students may be the stereotypical "coming-of-age" person (eighteen to twenty-five years old) or later-life learners. This cornucopia of possibilities is a tremendous strength, evidence that there is no one college that is best for every student. Rather, for each student there is a set of colleges that are "well suited." Ideally, within this array of possibilities, each student would be matched with the learning environment suited to him or her, and each student would go as far down the path of learning as his or her capacities permit. A college or university that is just perfect for one student could well be a disaster for another.

The differences that determine whether the match of a student with an institution is a good one go well beyond the academic specialty of the school (an aspiring mathematician should not go to Juilliard, just as an aspiring dancer should not go to Cal Tech), extending to more subtle factors such as the ethos of the school (competitive or cooperative); the mix of its students (graduate or undergraduate, older or younger, working or not); the setting (urban or rural); the size (large, medium, or small); and many other factors.

Each potential student is different—even if the two students in question live next door to each other, still more if they come from dramatically different circumstances. The informed and connected know this, as illustrated by the ritual—nearly compulsory in some social circles—of touring campuses as part of the application process in order to find the right fit of student and college. But as a society we have done an unacceptable job of matching students with the higher-education environment appropriate for them.

There is powerful evidence that we are allowing high-talent, college-ready students from lower socioeconomic groups to slip through the cracks—that is, to see high school graduation as the end of their time in school. A longitudinal study by the Education Trust, "Falling Out of the Lead" (2014), revealed that of the more than half a million students who scored in the top quartile nationally on a math and reading assessment, 23 percent of students with the lowest socioeconomic status did not even take the SAT or ACT exam, the standardized tests which are crucial to the college application process, compared to only 5 percent of similarly accomplished students with the highest socioeconomic status.[5]

Even those students from lower economic groups who do go to college are "undermatched." In *Crossing the Finish Line: Completing College at America's Public Universities,* Bill Bowen, former president of the Mellon Foundation and former president of Princeton University (writing with Matthew Chingos and Michael McPherson), demonstrated that students from the top economic quartile tend to be "overmatched" with colleges or universities (that is, they attend schools that offer a more advanced program than they merit, all factors being equal), but that students from the lower economic quartile are "undermatched" (they attend schools that offer a less advanced program than they merit).[6] Moreover, when students are "undermatched" with a school, they tend to perform less well than they would have performed if they had been properly matched. They miss out on key programs, are not pushed by a peer group of comparably gifted students, and become bored by the lack of challenge. Subsequent studies have confirmed these findings, and that the six-year graduation rate for students who undermatch is 28 percent lower than for those who matched well.[7]

To allow significant numbers of high-talent, college-ready students from low-income families to miss college altogether is a national tragedy. And undermatching, combined with further stratification of American higher education through stripped-down, low-cost programs of questionable quality, is an added threat to what many people seek in a college degree—social mobility and a solid financial future. In a diverse system, proper matching is the obverse of the fungibility fallacy: it deploys the different forms of higher education in service of maximizing talent development and should be a primary concern in public policy conversations about higher education.

There are four distinct factors involved in matching students with the school that is best for them. We must make sure, first, that there is a broad range of easily available, reliable, and transparent information upon which applicants can base their selections; second, that they have capable assistance in navigating the available information and the application process; third, that they perceive the importance of matching themselves with an educational environment most likely to develop their talents; and finally, that they obtain the resources to seize the opportunity they are offered.

Providing the Information to Facilitate Matching

Any sensible system designed to match prospective students with the higher education most likely to maximize their potential would offer clear, consistent, objective, and verified data on a standard list of matters of universal interest: tuition, net tuition, course offerings, class sizes, faculty/student ratios, faculty awards, student profile (SAT or ACT percentiles, standing in high school class, gender, nationality, race), placement ratios (for six months, a year, and five years after graduation), student satisfaction, and income of graduates in various programs (one, five, and ten years after graduation). Federal law now requires much of these data; but it must be available in standardized, easily accessible formats. And the data alone are not enough. If we are not careful, students and those who help them to make decisions about education will mistakenly think that only these data are relevant to the choice they are making.

A data system that provided only this relatively easily obtained information likely would create an incentive among some who run colleges and universities (not to their credit) to manipulate the behavior of the institution solely to "look better" on the criteria captured in the data chosen for collection—at the expense of other critically important elements that are more difficult to measure. For example, admissions officers might be encouraged to consider only standardized test scores (ignoring information on extracurricular activities or on personal background) in order to improve the median scores of the school; or they might be encouraged to use only stated grades (ignoring course difficulty) in order to improve on that criterion. Although creating a positive image for the school in the short term, these tactics would undermine in the long run the quality of the school's assessment of students in the entering class, ultimately thwarting the effort to match the right students with the right schools.

Some have proposed ranking colleges and universities by the "rate of return on investment" produced by their degrees. Presumably, proponents of such a ranking system would measure the "return" by the income of graduates. Although income information (by degree category, and at varying numbers of years after graduation) indeed should be part of the data publicized by every school, the idea of using such information for a ranking system is a diabolical one. The notion of measuring the value of a degree in these terms would be rejected by the likes of Newman and Pelikan—and surely by those, like me, who seek to advance the positive social aspect of universities.

It is important that the information we provide cover a broad spectrum (I call it a "dashboard"), beyond the obvious, measurable items. Fortunately, there are models already available that might capture some of the less quantifiable elements, which nevertheless should be available to students as they make their choices.

One such system, familiar to architects and builders, is the LEED system of rating buildings for environmental quality. In this program, builders voluntarily choose to meet best-practice standards at a level of quality, determined by an independently developed and informed point system. A building is rated platinum, gold, silver, or bronze according to these standards. This verified rating can then be advertised to attract to the building those who would prefer to live or locate businesses in an environmentally responsible building. An analogous system could be created for dozens of activities potentially important to prospective students. Peer panels could validate submissions by institutions interested in featuring a particular characteristic—rating them platinum, gold, silver, bronze, or unworthy of certification. The schools then could use the ratings as a dashboard picture of themselves to inform student choice. No school would secure ratings in all possible categories; and the absence of a rating could be taken to indicate that a school does not make any claim in that field. Combined with a list of standardized college data, such a school dashboard would paint a picture of the characteristics and priorities of participating schools, and students could determine whether those elements match their needs and interests.

Under this system, for example, NYU would feature (in addition to the obvious fact that it is a major research university in New York City) strong ratings for its study-away programs, its student wellness systems, its comprehensive career placement service, its extensive internship offerings, and, perhaps surprising to some, the balanced approach of its Division III athletic program, offering varsity competition against other strong academic schools. This list of characteristics would attract some students, while others who did not see themselves needing or utilizing such opportunities would think twice about coming to NYU, because its tuition would reflect the cost of the listed programs.

I would add one further element: As part of the accreditation peer-review process, each school would have to state its essential philosophy and purpose—its *ratio studiorum*—and how it aligns its various programs in service of that goal. As part of the existing periodic accreditation review process, the school would be asked to explain, with examples, how, in practice, it advances its stated goal. The reviewers would audit the stated evidence as part of their visit and grade the institution (again, platinum, gold, silver, bronze, or unworthy). Equipped with all this information, a student could make an informed choice, at least narrowing the field to a list of schools that would match well with his or her talents, desires, and passions.

To advance the capacity of all students, especially those with few resources, to use the provided information well, I propose an analogue to Teach for America. Call it "College Counselors for America," a corps of recent graduates, drawn in large measure from underrepresented communities, who would receive two- or three-year fellowships that place them in schools where they could provide needed college counseling. They could explain to students how a college education might make a difference in their lives; they could help students use all the available matching information, guide them through their applications for both admission and financial aid, and work through evaluating offers of admission and financial aid.

The beginnings of such a program already exist and have proved successful. Conceived and led by an extraordinary NYU graduate, Nicole Hurd, the College Advising Corps (CAC) places trained recent college graduates from partner institutions as full-time college advisers in underserved high schools. These advisers help students search for an appropriate college, complete admissions and financial aid applications, and see them through the final steps needed to complete enrollment. Close in age and background to the students they serve, they can connect with students in ways that others often cannot.

Since the program's launch at NYU in 2011, cohorts of NYU graduates have dedicated two years after graduation to CAC service. The results have been outstanding. Consider that in 2018, 86 percent of the students at NYU's forty-two partner high schools qualified for a free or reduced-price lunch.[8] Across all of NYU's partner high schools, 94 percent of graduating seniors submitted college applications and 80 percent of seniors had at least one college acceptance. Moreover, the NYU CAC advisers helped secure over $95 million in scholarships and institutional grant aid for their students.[9]

In all its partner schools, CAC has had a significant impact on matriculation and persistence to obtain a degree. One high school experienced a 71 percent increase in college enrollment in a single year; at another, enrollment doubled.[10] Nationally, 74 percent of the enrollees served by CAC persisted through their sophomore year, exceeding by a considerable margin the national rate for low-income students.[11]

These data are encouraging. But while CAC now has over 650 advisers in over 600 high schools, serving more than two hundred thousand students, the need is much larger. We need to scale this national effort if all our young people are to be encouraged to achieve their potential.

But we must do still more to increase the chances that every student can find the right school. In addition to initiatives like CAC that provide mentors, we should use technology and social media. For example, the U.S. Army, at its GoArmy.com website, features "Sergeant Star," who guides interested potential recruits through the process of choosing a career in the service. It is a sophisticated program that could be emulated in the college matching process.

Facing the Cost and Price of Higher Education

Once the student is matched with a college or university that is well suited for him or her, and the school has ratified that decision by expressing its interest, the price of attending the school becomes important. There is a lot of confusion about this topic.

First, the cost of education and the price (meaning the tuition or the cost of attendance) are not the same, and the distinction between them is important. Cost is the amount the school needs to deliver the education it offers; price is the amount charged to the student to cover, in part, the cost of what is delivered. In most of American higher education, and in most education systems around the world, the cost of what is provided exceeds the price that is charged, with the difference made up through some sort of subsidy—from government, from an allocation out of the school's endowment, or from current philanthropy. The exception is the for-profit sector, where the goal is to create a profit margin by keeping cost below price.

Second, in a functioning, complex economy, the cost of the most comprehensive forms of a college or university education would rise more rapidly than headline inflation; indeed, this is the mathematical outcome of a formula reflecting the differing impact of technology in the general economy (where it drives down cost quite dramatically) and in a high-talent service sector (where it has very little effect on costs). Two sophisticated formulations of this phenomenon are presented in the book *Why Does College Cost So Much?*[12] and in the American Council on Education's paper *The Anatomy of College Tuition*.[13] The essence of the argument is that the key components of a college or university education are the quality of the faculty and the degree of meaningful student exposure to faculty. Consequently, the greater the quality of the offerings, the more it costs to offer them. One example is the increased cost associated with lower faculty/student ratio.

Third, the price of education need not rise. Even in the face of rising costs for the various components of a quality education, tuition (price) can be restrained, either by introducing additional subsidies (a good idea) or by reducing quality (a bad idea).

Fourth, to the extent that the proposition about the inexorable rising cost of a quality college or university is supported by strong evidence, an iron triad rules. To maintain quality, either subsidy or tuition (price) must rise. To reduce tuition, either subsidy must rise or quality must diminish. And to reduce subsidy, either quality must fall or tuition must rise.

Fifth, the last four decades have seen a tectonic shift in the way our public policy views higher education, moving away from regarding it as a "public good" (as in the GI Bill or the early versions of the New York State Regents Scholarship) toward seeing it as a "private good" (the students who benefit should bear the full cost of the education provided). In policy terms, the result has been a reduction in the public subsidy provided for higher education, with the cost shifting to individuals. This shift combines with the upward pressure on costs to accelerate the rise in price (tuition).

Sixth, as in every sector, there are inefficiencies in higher education. Anecdotes that highlight outrageous cases abound, and often dominate the conversation. All unnecessary expenditures must be eliminated, but as universities work to root them out, they must take care to avoid damaging programs that are actually increasing effectiveness—programs that indeed come with added cost but are not examples of inefficiency. For example, student wellness programs may add expense but they also may increase retention. American higher education is highly competitive—both internally and externally. Our colleges and universities already strive to be as efficient as possible. There may be gains to be made, to be sure, but those who expect a bonanza will be disappointed.

Seventh, in pursuing a college or university education, students may be willing to sacrifice elements of the most comprehensive college or university education in order to lower their cost of attendance. Without a scholarship or other aid, some will be forced by their financial circumstances to make that choice. We make such choices with most purchases, and we do it often with expensive purchases such as houses, automobiles, vacations, or appliances.

In search of a lower price, an individual student might well *choose to* forgo schools with one or more of the following: a richer curriculum, a lower faculty-student ratio, an extensive tutorial/mentoring ethos, a robust set of international programs, a rich co-curricular program, a carefully developed student wellness service, a strong placement office, a diverse student body (the product of a searching and therefore well-staffed admissions process and generous financial aid packages), or quality facilities (from labs to dorms to athletic facilities)—to name a few relevant factors. For some students, some of these elements may be unimportant and, therefore, not worth the additional price. For these students, sacrificing such factors for a lower price might make complete sense.

Yet others—and a just society should want as few of these as possible—may be forced by the higher cost of attendance to sacrifice elements they see as potentially important to their full development. We ought to worry about these cases. The privileged who need not consider price rarely choose to sacrifice the quality of their education in order to save money. In New York, for example, many parents invest enormous effort in enrolling their children in K–12 programs that cost $40,000 a year or more, and they often spend considerable additional money for tutoring and counseling services so that their children can choose to attend a higher-price college or university.

In sum, especially in the knowledge century, society has a significant interest in maximizing the level of every citizen's development, which is why we should strive to minimize the number of cases where a student is forced by price to accept less than optimal development of his or her talent. This case inevitably requires a subsidy to bridge the gap between the price and the ability of the student to pay for it. And as tuition goes up, the subsidy also increases.

The Role of Technology

As technology permeates our society—disrupting sectors as diverse as publishing and transportation—many commentators argue that American higher education is caught in an "old model" that has not adapted to this new, very different environment. According to these critics, the preeminence of American higher education is its weakness, leaving those in charge of our colleges and universities complacent, bound to be surpassed by foreign competitors or new delivery methods. This was the fate of the American auto industry in the 1970s.

But, the leaders of American higher education are anything but complacent. Competition within the sector for talent is fierce, and the impetus for innovation is very strong. Complacency is the last emotion to prevail in the halls of academe. Whether through research or the development of new delivery mechanisms, the major innovations in integrating technology into education have been born on American campuses.

There is no doubt that, in the coming decades, technology will play an increasingly important role at all levels of education, including higher education. In some areas, as in the general economy, it will help drive down costs, which should be reflected in price. Some degrees will be offered wholly online at dramatically reduced cost and price. For some students, especially older or working students, an online college degree may be the best match. As far as I know, nobody in higher education is resisting these truths.

However, as we embrace technology, we must integrate it appropriately into our diverse higher-education system. Quality must be the lodestar, and context matters.

Today, and still more in the years to come, various courses will be enhanced by the introduction of technology before, during, or after the traditional interaction between a professor and students. Some courses will be supplemented with simulations and games made possible by technology. Other courses, using technology, will take place in multiple sites, simultaneously or asynchronously, creating a richer curriculum by introducing dimensions or experts not otherwise available. Each of these developments is significant, each contributing to the quality of education in some way. While some innovations will lower costs, others will add costs, but the increase will be worth it because the educational outcome is better or more widely available.

Although it may seem counterintuitive, in colleges and universities that serve the most advanced students and have the most talented faculty, technology adds to the overall cost, even after netting savings against costs. This is largely because it is important to train students in the use of the very latest technological tools, and it is vitally important to provide those tools to advanced researchers. This demand drives a cycle of investment and rapid depreciation on many campuses—an investment that drives up cost. So technology is not a silver bullet that can be used to lower cost; in important parts of the sector, it drives higher cost.

Perhaps the greatest immediate impact of technology (seen, for example, in the emergence of the massive open online courses or MOOCs) is the possibility of bringing education to vast numbers of people through the internet. It is in this modality that attention to "quality in context" is important.

I am chairman of the President's Council for the University of the People, an online university created and run by a visionary man, Shai Reshef. The University of the People admits any student who has a high school diploma, is fluent in English, and has internet access. Students take classes in relatively small sections—usually two or three dozen students per class—using open-source material in curricula developed and guided by volunteer professors. At the end of the course, each student takes a secure exam and receives a grade. The University of the People is now an accredited American university (by the Distance Education and Training Council). Except for a modest exam fee, which the University of the People waives upon request, the education is free.

The first time I saw Shai present his university, a technology enthusiast who was moderating the panel exclaimed: "You are the future!" Shai responded: "I hope not. We are simply the source of hope for those for whom the alternative is nothing."

Context is key: Even the bare-bones approach provided by the University of the People is better than no education at all. If we can avoid it, however, we should not relegate talented young people to a bare-bones education. Shai and I have started a program that helps students who show special promise in their first courses in the University of the People to make their way, with financial aid, to comprehensive universities. Already, Berkeley, Edinburgh, and NYU have found extraordinary students through this approach.

Online education can be an important tool, bringing higher education to millions who might otherwise not be able to obtain it. It might provide an education to others who have access in theory to a college or university education but who, as a practical matter, cannot pursue a traditional course of study. Some have a job that must take priority over classes offered at times that will not work with their employment; others have family obligations; still others live in remote places. The use of technology in these cases will be an important part of the "massification" and "democratization" of higher education.

Which brings me to a final point about the use of technology in higher education. If we stay aware of the danger of a socially disastrous segregation, we can take steps to use technology as a search engine to discover academically gifted students and make it possible for them to move up a ladder of opportunity. Just as the University of the People has identified talented students who, given the opportunity and adequate financial assistance, could thrive at Berkeley, Edinburgh, or NYU, so too technology-driven courses and MOOCs could help find talented students all over the world. It therefore is necessary that the courses offered through technology be accompanied by processes that spot talent and that financial aid programs be available to the students so identified to provide ladders of opportunity for all.

There is nothing wrong with "a $10,000 college degree," so long as it is freely chosen by students who are aware how different it is from a degree that costs $180,000. But a bare-bones education should not be forced on someone who could flourish with a more comprehensive education. There is no way to experience Charlie, my high school teacher, online. Our efforts to increase the number of citizens with college degrees will not be successful—no matter what the numbers show—unless each citizen is given a chance to realize his or her full potential.

The Misleading Rhetoric about Tuition and Student Debt

Over the years, as commentators have focused on the phenomenon of rising tuition, "facts" only loosely tethered to reality have become embedded in the public conversation. Since one consequence is a loss of hope and a false sense that a college or university education is beyond many Americans, it is useful to lay out the data on tuition and student debt trends for undergraduate education. The numbers are surprising to most, because we have been conditioned to apply adjectives like "exorbitant," "shocking," "staggering," and "crushing" to student debt.

Politicians of both parties at all levels of government commonly have focused on the need for price reductions in higher education without acknowledging the concomitant negative effect of such reductions on quality. Indeed, this focus permeates the conversation on higher education as shaped by the experts and pundits, a few of whom have built careers attacking higher education.

Their first contention, buttressed by stories about rock-climbing walls and lazy rivers, is that colleges and universities are "gold plating" their facilities and services to attract students. They then proceed with a claim that campuses are rife with inefficiencies—administrative bloat, undue support for faculty research, and other unchecked spending. Their argument continues with an assertion that colleges and universities will spend whatever tuition or government assistance they receive and not restrain costs if left to themselves. And it concludes with the prophecy that the higher education "bubble" is about to burst.

Isolated anecdotes aside, this explanation for rising tuition is at odds with the reality of life within a college or university. First, one person's "gold plating" is someone else's essential component; such is the reality of a system that offers a wide variety of choice. From orientation programs to placement services, from classics courses to small-group seminars, any element of a school's offerings could be judged by someone to be "gold plating." The same element could be the key to a student's success in studies and in life. Each enrichment adds cost and, absent subsidy, raises tuition. Yet, for a particular student, that one offering and consequent tuition increase may be the difference between the school that will fulfill his or her potential and one that will not.

Second, while no doubt there are inefficiencies on college and university campuses, most have engaged in aggressive efforts to minimize their administrative costs. At NYU, we reduced university administrative costs 20 percent, through a set of measures ranging from energy cost reduction (NYU now has its own cogeneration plant) to eliminating duplicative administrative functions. True, the total number of administrators on campuses is higher than it was two or three decades ago, but this increase most often is due to a commendable increase in attention given to important new programs (like student wellness and health services) or to the dramatically increased regulatory and compliance demands imposed by government.

At this point, the critics of higher education usually switch to a third argument. They claim that in higher education, as in health care, the presence of a third-party payer—in higher education, the government through grants and loans; in health care, the public or private insurer—eliminates the incentive for providers to restrain costs. But, in health care, those who decide to spend more (the doctor and the patient) do not pay the marginal increase in price; third-party payers do. In higher education, by contrast, those who decide to spend more to attend one college rather than another (the students and their families) pay the lion's share of the increase—either immediately or through loan repayments. Because students and their families are concerned about what they will pay for higher education, it is important for the institutions to restrain price as much as possible without damaging quality in order to win the competition for talent.

At this point, the critics enter a fourth stage, with a prediction: that those in the higher-education sector will soon see the "bubble" burst, because students and their families will not continue to pay the ever-increasing price of attendance. Those who offer this prophecy usually allude to the dot-com bubble, the housing bubble, or the tulip bubble that preceded them centuries ago. This kind of talk is especially ill-conceived. Past financial and commodity bubbles were the result of speculation:

Investors purchased stocks and homeowners borrowed funds to purchase an asset on the speculative assumption that it would increase in value so that it later could be resold at a price sufficient to repay the borrowing and deliver a profit. In a bubble, the process feeds on itself for a time but then stops, with a dramatic decline in value; ultimately, the investor or borrower is "underwater" because the speculation proves to be unfounded.

In no way is student borrowing analogous to such ventures. Students do not earn a degree in order to resell it to someone else. Education is a good in itself, a lifetime benefit. Moreover, to the extent there is an interest in monetizing the value of a degree (into lifetime earnings, for example), the return on investment is not speculative but rather easily ascertainable from available data on placement in various career paths. A dance major embraces different earning prospects from a business major, but with clear data and good guidance, the dancer can make an informed choice, not a speculative bet.

In the end, those who study the data know that a higher education is important, that it creates the predicate for a more successful life, and that it positively affects lifetime earnings. Indeed, according to an analysis by the Economic Policy Institute, the pay gap between college graduates and others has continued to grow over time—and now is at a record level.[14]

Yet while most Americans understand that a home is a capital investment, they do not view higher education in the same way. This confusion is especially troubling because the value of a home (as we were reminded in 2009) can drop quickly, while the value of an appropriately chosen college or university education never diminishes—whether we measure the value of the education narrowly as economic gain or more broadly as a path to a fulfilling life.

The popular framing of the issue exacerbates the confusion, especially among those who are less financially sophisticated. Much is made of the fact that America's total debt for higher education has passed its total credit card debt, truly a comparison of apples and horses. Credit card debt is consumer spending, not capital investment. By contrast, total borrowing for higher education is far less than mortgage borrowing, a much more comparable category of debt.

In other words, "experts" are telling Americans that it is sensible to assume a $250,000 mortgage (and additional monthly maintenance charges) to buy a small one-bedroom apartment in one of the outer boroughs of New York City, but somehow unwise to assume significantly less indebtedness for a college education.

However, not only is the framing of the issues flawed; often, the facts are wrong or misleading.

Consider the conventional discussion of tuition. True, tuition levels—the "sticker price" of full tuition—have been increasing, in most schools more rapidly than headline (CPI) inflation, an understandable situation given the nature of higher education and the reduction in subsidy provided by the government and other sources. Adjusted for inflation, however, the actual numbers are not nearly as dramatic as most would guess: Over the last ten years, nominal tuition (plus fees) at four-year public universities has risen 37 percent; over the last five years, 8 percent; over the last two years, 3 percent.[15] The comparable numbers at four-year private universities are 26 percent (ten years), 12 percent (five years), and 4.5 percent (two years).[16]

Of course, many students do not pay full tuition. Often, they receive a subsidy in the form of a financial aid grant, resulting in the net tuition these students actually pay. For a more accurate picture, one must look at the trends in net tuition.

Here, increases at public universities, reflecting the reductions in government support, are still significant: 35 percent (ten years); 20 percent (five years); and 9 percent (two years). In private, not-for-profit colleges and universities, however, the picture is very different. Net tuition actually has decreased over the last ten years by 8 percent. According to the College Board, the average student at a private college or university today pays only 57 percent of the price listed for tuition, room, and board (down from 67 percent ten years ago), resulting in a net price in tuition, adjusted for inflation, that is lower at such schools than a decade earlier.[17] These facts are certainly not what you will read in most papers.

Similarly, the magnitude of student debt is also not as dire as reported. According to a 2015 Federal Reserve Bank of New York report, 43 percent of student debtors owed a total of less than $10,000; 65 percent, less than $20,000; and 95 percent, less than $100,000.[18]

Two books—Sandy Baum, *Student Debt: Rhetoric and Realities of Higher Education Financing,* and Beth Akers and Matthew M. Chingos, *Game of Loans: The Rhetoric and Reality of Student Debt*—offer comprehensive analyses of student borrowing that lead to conclusions very much at odds with the conventional wisdom that there is a "student debt crisis."[19] Both books note that families in the top-earning quartile hold half of student debt; families in the top 10 percent of earners hold a quarter of the debt; and those holding the highest amount of student debt have a higher proportion of advanced and professional degrees and have lower default rates. In short, the wealthiest among us have the greatest amount of student debt— and they can repay it. Somewhat surprisingly, as a group, borrowers who default have borrowed less on average than those in good standing; and by far the greatest number of defaulting students are among those who attend relatively low-priced, for-profit schools. A Brookings study finds that many for-profit students would be better off not attending college at all. On average, for-profit certificate students do not generate enough earnings to offset the debt they incur.[20]

The most serious problem is among students with student loans for higher education who do not complete the degrees for which they borrow. They are left with debt and without a degree, the worst of both worlds. Not surprisingly, these students most often attended for-profit schools or not-for-profit schools with fairly observable records of mediocrity—low completion rates, low placement records, low scores in student satisfaction, and weak peer reviews. This finding underscores the importance of good guidance that matches students with schools where they are likely to succeed.

Even without aggressive efforts to match students well, the data show that for the great majority a college or university education is one of the very best investments. Putting aside the important but unmeasurable enhancements to quality of life and judged in merely economic returns, the return on investment is enormous. In 2014, MIT economist David Autor estimated that the true cost of a college degree (tuition/fees minus the gap in lifetime earnings) is negative $500,000, adjusted for inflation and the time value of money.[21] With the record college pay gap, the value today is even greater than it was decades ago.

Moreover, what economists call the opportunity cost of attending college—or, to put it in lay terms, the amount of income forfeited by a student who continues school rather than taking a job—is declining, because there are fewer jobs for those who do not attend college and the jobs that are available to them pay less. Thus, as the opportunity cost continues to fall, and the earning potential of a college degree continues to rise, the true cost of a college degree continues to decrease.

Faced with these numbers, those who warn us of a "student debt crisis" go on to introduce a new argument: Students who borrow fare less well in life than others, even if they do not default. To support this assertion, they cite the inaugural Gallup-Purdue Index Report, a study of the life outcomes of more than thirty thousand college graduates. The relevant section, titled "Loan Debt Can Cripple Well-Being," states: "The amount of student loans that graduates take out to pay for their undergraduate degree is related to their well-being in every element. The higher the loan amount, the worse the well-being."[22]

This sounds compelling—until you notice the groups it is comparing: one group of college graduates who borrowed versus another group who did not borrow, with the most significant differences occurring in a comparison of those who borrowed more than $50,000 (about 2 percent of all graduates) and those who left school with no student debt (about 43 percent). The results of this comparison are just common sense: Across various dimensions of well-being, those who have no debt tend to feel better than those who have debt, and those with no debt tend to feel particularly better than those with the greatest debt. To say the least, this conclusion is not surprising. The question should not be whether students would be better off if they had the dollars they borrowed in their pocket, but whether they are better off with student debt and the degree for which it paid than they would be without the debt or the degree. The evidence is overwhelming that students are better off with both the debt and the degree.

Some findings of the survey are notable in that they discount the effect of debt: For instance, those with debt were about as likely to say they were "thriving socially" as those with no debt. And one finding of the survey is especially informative: The major factor in later-life well-being reported by graduates was a connection with a professor on campus who encouraged them—some equivalent of Charlie in my own life. Graduates with such an experience were three times more likely to "thrive"—as were all graduates who had done a seminar project or who were very involved in extracurricular activities. This finding should give pause to those who discount the importance of a high-quality faculty, small classes, or out-of-class activities (with the attendant costs).

Uncorrected, the misconceptions about the fundamental issues surrounding the true cost of attendance, the nature and effects of student debt, and the value of a college degree will not only compromise the level of fulfillment of the students who are misled and discouraged, but also diminish our nation's prospects. As a Brookings Institution report noted in warning about disseminating potentially misleading information on student debt, "negative attitudes toward debt have the potential to encourage debt aversion, which can prevent students from enrolling in college in the first place."[23] Even for those who do enroll in college, the negative narrative might discourage them from attending the college or university that is the best match for them.

A Chinese friend once explained to me that in Confucian societies, the education of the next generation is the primary obligation for families and government, with homes, automobiles, and vacations as secondary. But, he said, in America, public policy assigns education to a lower status than one or even all three of these other priorities. He is right at least in part: One leading policy maker recently lamented that a graduate who is carrying the average $28,000 in student loans would be forced to defer the purchase, presumably on a loan of roughly the same amount, of a car. In a way, the issue of the cost of higher education is only a special version of the tendency of Americans to value short-term benefits over long-term rewards. But in this century, when the success of societies will depend on the educational attainment of their citizens, it is a particularly troubling manifestation. Public policy must respond—and must put funding behind the effort. We now turn to that issue.

Mitigating the Burden of Student Debt: Income-Based Repayment

Those blessed with the kind of talents that merit advanced education are not concentrated in any single zip code or social class, whether defined by income, gender, race, or ethnicity. Our policy makers must therefore be particularly sensitive to any tendency to confine the benefits of higher education to those born to privilege. Society cannot afford to squander talent, wherever it is. A recent report from the New America Foundation found that nearly two-thirds of selective public colleges and universities enroll fewer students from low-income families than they did twenty years ago—with a nearly identical increase in enrollment from students coming from top-income families.[24]

In an ideal world, higher education would be seen as a public good, a right available to all who could benefit from it. In many developed countries that view predominates, but it no longer animates policy in the United States. Given this unfortunate truth, the best way to make the appropriate college or university education available to every qualified student is an income-based repayment program. If properly designed, such a program should give students confidence that they could borrow money from the government to finance a quality degree from the school best suited to them without facing an undue financial burden after graduation.

Versions of income-based repayment programs already exist in Australia and the United Kingdom. Two comprehensive studies—the Browne Report and Hamilton Project—present nuanced and comprehensive versions of this type of plan. Other alternatives can be developed, and I will later suggest a number of possible modifications. These plans, and the one I will propose, are affordable and make economic sense.

Pay as You Earn (PAYE), as developed by the Obama administration in 2012, could become the foundation for an effective income-based loan repayment program. The program's structure is straightforward. Students who borrow do so in a standard government loan program and repay the loans after graduation. However (and here is the major feature of the program), the amount students are required to pay during any year is capped at the lower of two numbers: either 10 percent of income above a set level (presently, 150 percent of the state poverty level) or the amount that would have been owed under a standard full-recourse loan with a ten-year period. After twenty years of payments, the remaining balance is discharged. In 2015, the Department of Education expanded the PAYE program to allow more borrowers to qualify (Revised Pay as You Earn, or REPAYE).[25]

Ordinarily, a graduate with $50,000 of debt upon graduation would be required to pay roughly $6,500 annually during the standard ten-year repayment period. If that same student were enrolled in the PAYE program, the debt service would be based on the parameters of the program described above but would never exceed $6,500. However, the cap might lower payments: For example, at 150 percent of the current New York State poverty level ($18,090 for an individual), a hypothetical graduate with an adjusted gross income of $26,090 would pay only $800 (that is, 10 percent of the $8,000 above $18,090) instead of $6,500.[26]

State plans can be a valuable supplement. New York State has the Get on Your Feet Loan Forgiveness Program, which allows New York residents who graduate from college and continue to live in the state to pay little or nothing of their student loans for the first two years out of school if their income is not high enough to cover their student debt burden. New York's program supplements the federal PAYE program to make it still easier for graduates to manage their student loan payments. For students who continue to live in the state following graduation and who participate in the PAYE program, New York State will cover 100 percent of their student loan payments for two years if they earn less than $50,000 a year. By combining the PAYE program with New York's supplementary assistance, eligible students will not have to make any payments on student loans for the first two years after college.[27]

Echoing the conversation about student debt, some critics charge that the greater availability of debt from income-based repayment programs simply helps to drive rising tuition. Others suggest that such programs might discourage borrowing for other important purchases, such as a home. And still others charge that these income-based loan plans create a "moral hazard" by encouraging students to take on debt with the expectation that they will not need to repay it.

These arguments are remarkably paternalistic in depriving the "protected" students of important choices that could improve their lives. Even with an ambitious income-based loan repayment program, schools would still have a strong incentive to provide as much financial aid as possible to compete successfully for the best students. And students would continue to be motivated to borrow as little as possible, since if they borrow less, their loan payments will be lower. Colleges and universities will still have to justify higher tuition to prospective students and donors by demonstrating that they provide additional value.

As noted earlier, some will choose to forgo educational amenities in favor of spending or borrowing less, just as consumers do all the time. It is particularly important, however, that when it comes to choosing an education such a choice be informed and voluntary—that is, not dictated by economic or social class.

The process of matching and sorting, if supported by adequate access to key information and adequate funding and financial aid mechanisms such as those just described, will over time have profound effects on the shape of the American higher-education landscape. Schools where tuition is seen as too high, given their value proposition, will suffer. High-tuition, high-quality schools with an articulated, significant value proposition will survive and thrive; but such schools will be accessible to all whose talents are suited to them. The higher-education sector will be tailored to the choices of students and their families—none of whom will be trapped by circumstance.

There is one final argument against income-based repayment plans that deserves extended discussion: that the PAYE program and programs like it will impose substantial added costs on the federal government. The total cost of the present PAYE program for undergraduate loans, even without increases, is not yet clear. What is clear is that the number of borrowers entering the PAYE program is rising. Today the 6.5 million borrowers in the program represent 25 percent of all borrowers, they hold $352 billion in total debt, and their debt constitutes about half of all student debt currently in repayment.[28] But those who stand to gain the most are not yet taking full advantage of it.

Since income-based loan repayment programs represent the policy most likely to allow students to attend the college suited to them, I view an increase in PAYE participation as a desirable goal. Clearly, however, increased participation will raise the cost of the program. But the resources can be found.

Taken as a whole (and without counting the enormous indirect economic benefits), government-provided student loans with income-contingent repayment provisions could be seen as paying for themselves. In 2012, when the government eliminated private lenders and became the provider of student loans, it garnered an annual profit of $40 billion.[29] It is only fair that some of this profit be used to cover the cost of a generous income-contingent repayment plan. In addition to recapturing these resources, a sufficiently generous income-contingent repayment program would allow redirection of monies currently devoted to an array of federal grants that arguably would no longer be necessary; this reallocation alone could cover the increased cost.

Moreover, to the extent that the PAYE program and other, perhaps more generous programs like it are more costly to taxpayers than existing loan programs, policy makers could consider adopting changes to the structure of the PAYE program that would have a relatively modest impact on most borrowers but could significantly reduce the aggregate amount of loan write-offs. Such changes might include: relaxing the cap that limits monthly debt service on income-based repayments to the level they would be under traditional loan repayment programs; extending the repayment period from twenty years to twenty-five years; and basing repayment on household income as opposed to individual income.

There are other ways to lower potential costs, such as implementing a two-tiered loan forgiveness horizon based on initial loan balance, with loan balances under $40,000 forgiven after twenty years and loan balances equal to or greater than $40,000 forgiven after twenty-five years; eliminating the payment cap that currently restricts monthly payments to no more than what would be owed under the standard ten-year repayment plan, even if 10 percent of discretionary income exceeds this amount; or instituting a loan forgiveness cap for the Public Service Loan Forgiveness program of $57,500.[30]

Further variations are possible. My own preferred way to limit the overall cost of the program for the government is by setting basic performance standards for colleges and universities before they become eligible to certify graduates for income-based loans. Standards might include minimum graduation rates (for example, 70 percent of the national average). That minimum could be lowered for schools that admit and benefit lower-income, underrepresented, or at-risk students. Well-designed minimum requirements would hasten the demise of the schools that today deliver little to students other than debt (usually, debt in exchange for a meaningless degree or no degree at all). The elimination of such schools would lower default rates and thus the costs of the program.

A combination of the various cost savings I have listed could support an income-based repayment model that would cover borrowing (up to a cap) at substantially higher levels than the borrowing covered by the PAYE program. For example, a cap set at the 80th percentile of tuition in the private university sector would allow students true freedom to match with the schools best for them.

For now, the optimal income-contingent repayment plan is still "to be determined." The main point is this: If we accept that the United States will no longer provide, as a public good, the cost of an appropriately matched higher education to its citizens, then a well-developed income-based repayment program that treats higher education as a "quasi" public good would go a long way to creating the possibility that each American could maximize his or her potential and opportunities.

A Case Study in Applying the Proposal: NYU

NYU is an elite, tuition-dependent research university, the largest private university in the United States. Fewer than 40 years ago, it accepted almost every student who applied—and was on the verge of bankruptcy. Indeed, faculty and staff were once asked to wait two weeks for their salary checks. NYU then had very few residential students; most students commuted from their homes in New York City and surrounding counties.

In 1981, under the extraordinary leadership of John Brademas and Jay Oliva, a transformation began that decades later Berkeley's David Kirp called "*the* success story in contemporary American higher education."[31] Today, NYU is one of the world's leading research universities.

The admissions process for all three portal campuses is driven by a desire to ensure that NYU is the best match for the individual student. Admissions officers explain carefully that NYU is a research university, with all that means for an undergraduate education. They note the differences among the three portals that might be more or less attractive to a given student. If a student is inclined toward our New York campus, they emphasize the variation in offerings among the twelve undergraduate schools—from traditional liberal arts schools, to an individualized-study liberal arts track, to the performing arts, to business, and so on.

In all cases, admission is "need-blind." Students are admitted without reference to their ability to pay. Once a student is admitted, however, if savvy admissions officers fear that his or her debt burden (based on likely borrowing, factoring in both government and institutional aid) will be at the upper range, they work to ensure that the student understands the financial ramifications of a decision to attend NYU—even if the result is that NYU sometimes does not enroll students it would love to have.

NYU tuition is the same whether a student enters through New York, Abu Dhabi, or Shanghai. However, the financial aid available is different, depending on the site. And the story behind that difference is revealing. In Abu Dhabi and in Shanghai, NYU partners with the government. Fortunately, the governmental partners in those countries embrace the notion that the education offered at NYU is a public good—and they provide resources to ensure that no student who should come to NYU Abu Dhabi or NYU Shanghai is prevented from doing so by his or her financial circumstances.

By contrast, NYU New York depends largely on the tuition paid by students to support its programs, including financial aid for the students less able to pay. The result is that many who need financial aid do not receive it at the level justified by their need. This contrast among the three campuses provides a vivid illustration of the cost (quality), subsidy, and price (tuition) equation in a tuition dependent research university. So, NYU's New York campus is a useful example of how the proposed program of income-based loan repayment would work.

Today, NYU's tuition is among the highest in the country (top 5 percent), despite yeoman efforts to restrain it as much as possible without compromising quality. With the added cost of room and board in New York, the full price of attendance for a residential student moves NYU even farther up the list. But, because NYU students often work while going to school to minimize their indebtedness, the actual figures on indebtedness for the vast majority of students are lower than the anecdotes in the media indicate.

For the most recent graduating class for which data are available, the median total debt (for the entire New York class) after four years was $2,750. If only students with loan debt are considered, eliminating those with zero debt, the median debt after four years rises to $26,885. At the seventy-fifth percentile, four-year debt is $26,888 for the full class and $32,809 for those students with loans. At the ninetieth percentile, the numbers are $36,537 and $57,505. At the ninety-fifth percentile, $57,542 and $84,625. In short, the extreme stories reported in the public discourse about student debt represent a tiny proportion of the class.

These numbers have not bred complacency on our campus. NYU has made funding still more generous financial aid a top priority. My successor, Andrew Hamilton, cares passionately about this. Yet the school's endowment still displays the effects of the university's brush with insolvency a mere two generations ago. Despite the university's standing and its remarkable fundraising success—the university has raised over $1 million a day, 365 days a year, for the last fifteen years—NYU's per-student endowment (the relevant number when isolating funds available for financial aid to students) is below the median for all private colleges and universities in the United States and is far below any of its peer schools.

Since 2003, NYU has nearly tripled its per capita endowment to $80,000 per student. At Harvard, Princeton, and Yale, this per-student figure approaches $2 million. At the traditional 5 percent rate of spending from endowment, the NYU endowment yields $4,000 per student; the comparable numbers at Harvard, Princeton, and Yale exceed $100,000 per student each year. These basic numbers mean that endowment support for financial aid at NYU New York is paltry, especially when compared to our peers.

The university does all it can to fight the consequences of this math. Annually, NYU provides well over $300 million in grant aid to its students. Of course, this allocation adds to the university's expense budget, but all students benefit from the presence of a more diverse class. The wealthiest students may benefit most by being exposed to peers who come from very different backgrounds and/or have to work a job in order to attend class.

In 2003, NYU offset only 34 percent of the demonstrated need of its students; today it offsets over 70 percent. But the university needs at least twice the current grant aid to provide New York students with the level of assistance offered by peer institutions blessed with endowments that have been built over generations and centuries—or the level of assistance given by NYU Abu Dhabi and NYU Shanghai. There is a lesson, however, in the math of tuition-driven financial aid. Stated in the most simplistic terms: If NYU were to hold its tuition at $40,000 instead of $45,000, it would be awarding the equivalent of a $5,000 scholarship to the child of the wealthiest family in the school (as well as all other students, of course). Were it to raise tuition to $45,000 and use the difference ($5,000) to fund scholarships for the poorest 80 percent of the class, the wealthiest 20 percent of the class would pay the extra fee while (on average) the poorer 80 percent of the class would receive a scholarship of $6,350, leaving them $1,350 better. This is the way tuition-funded financial aid works. And these numbers reveal the pernicious effect of "capping" or "flatlining" tuition (absent an increase in subsidy)—or of tossing encomiums at those who do.

Fortunately, the relative inadequacy of NYU's financial aid has not discouraged students—even financially challenged students—from choosing NYU. In the most recent entering class, 22 percent of NYU undergraduates were eligible for Pell Grants; the comparable numbers at peer schools tend to cluster between 11 percent and 14 percent. Nineteen percent of NYU undergraduates were the first in their family to attend college. At NYU's Tandon School of Engineering, just under 40 percent of this year's class are first-generation college students. These students really want to be at NYU, and many of them make it happen by working while attending. Thirty percent of NYU's undergraduates work two jobs, and about 12 percent work three. These statistics speak volumes about the value these students see in an NYU education. Most could have attended another school on a full scholarship or a lower net tuition. But they want what the children of the most advantaged in our society want: to attend the school that is best suited to their passions and talents.

I worry, however, that students who work so much will not able to take maximum advantage of the university—enrolling in all the classes they would like to take, not just those compatible with their work schedules; joining clubs and teams; and taking a semester or two at one of our study-away sites. With an income-based loan program, these students and their families could use government loans to pay for their NYU education, knowing the repayment of debt incurred would be limited to 10 percent of their discretionary income. They would then be able to take full advantage of that education, just as their wealthier classmates do.

In such a world, the financially well-off would pay the full amount. The school, to attract the best students with the widest possible life experiences, would provide enough financial aid to some students to cover the amount they have to pay, to the extent possible. Some of the poorest would likely receive enough financial aid to bring the amount to zero. From the student's standpoint, if a proposal along the lines discussed here were in effect, repayment obligations would be income contingent for all but 5 percent of NYU students. No student would have to pass up an NYU education if it were best for him or her.

The Cry of the World's Millions

Since I returned to NYU's faculty in January 2016, I have devoted much of my time to addressing the shameful fact that there are nearly 60 million school age children in the world who are out of school.[32] To these dismal numbers, add over 10 million displaced youth (every ten seconds another child is displaced) who had been in school but whose education was interrupted (and likely will not be resumed) while they remain displaced.[33] Once children reach a refugee camp, they stay for an average of ten years. So, for example, there are hundreds of thousands of children among the Syrian refugees in Turkey, Lebanon, and Jordan who were in primary and secondary school before the civil war but who are not in school today;[34] and there are over a hundred thousand older Syrian refugee children worldwide who are college-ready but who are not being educated.[35]

This crisis is an incomprehensible and morally indefensible calamity of wasted talent and failure of access. These numbers in aggregate represent a significant percentage of humanity— over half a billion children. The world cannot afford to lose this generation of young people. And this problem is not like cancer or climate change, where the cure or solution must be discovered. We know very well how to provide education to children.

Nor is cost an obstacle, or at least it should not be. When the G-20 leaders met in Hamburg in July 2017, they agreed to support the international financing plan advanced by former UK Prime Minister Gordon Brown. In global terms, a small amount of money—estimated at $10 billion annually in international aid, about half the aid currently allocated for health—could support major advances in primary and secondary education worldwide. This amount is less than a day's worth of the military spending of the UN's member countries; it is less than the cost of a single aircraft carrier.[36]

Should we succeed in providing primary and secondary schooling to these hundreds of millions of neglected children, the next challenge will be to make available college and graduate education to those eager to continue. Now is the time to begin preparing for this surge. Technology can play an important role in that next stage; indeed, it must play such a role, to handle the influx of millions (and, hopefully, tens of millions) of additional new students. Programs like the University of the People show the way. But those who develop systems based on technology to deliver a college education worldwide should take care to include a possibility for students who begin their education online but demonstrate a capacity that might merit their climbing a "ladder up" to a more comprehensive education. To create such a possibility is more complicated than teaching the children of the world to read and write, but we must find a way for this generation and those who will follow if we are to leave our descendants a more just world.

Empowering All in the Creation of an Ecumenical World

For fourteen years, I was privileged to serve as the president of a great university and, along the way, to serve on and chair the boards of several of higher education's major organizations. As a president who taught four courses each academic year and who loves students, I have gotten to know thousands of NYU students and their families. I can report that the presidents of our nation's colleges and universities join students and their families in desiring the finest possible education for students at the lowest possible cost. By and large, presidents strive to discover the ideas that will liberate funds for financial aid, stronger faculty, and the many new programs that become necessary as knowledge expands and new fields are created. University presidents are mission-driven, and their mission is to facilitate the advance of knowledge and to produce as many graduates as possible who experience it and its joys.

I have tried to explain the elements of a system that would increase the numbers of those who benefit from the magnificent incubating capacity of our colleges and universities. With modest investment of additional resources from the government, this system would match students with the college or university education most likely to maximize their advancement and provide a sensible way for them and society to finance it. If we were to adopt such a system, we would renew our traditional commitment to the idea that higher education is a public good that should be available to every citizen who can benefit from it.

It is not enough for our universities to provide an antidote to secular dogmatism; it is not enough even if they create a world in which secular ecumenism thrives. We also must demand of them and of the societies they nurture that all who have the requisite talent and desire be given the opportunity to reach the plateaus of achievement and happiness that education uniquely offers. Only if this is so will it be that all have voice in the ecumenical discourse.

Conclusion
Being Worthy of Lisa

To close, let me return to the beginning.

My first introduction to the world of meaningful dialogue came through competitive debate, a universe where ideas, logic, and intellectual encounter ruled. I was then privileged to witness the impact of this kind of dialogue in the movement from triumphalism to ecumenism among a group of religious leaders and theologians who utterly transformed the worldview of any who followed their path.

I know that such dialogue—grounded in the understanding that humankind is bound together in a common enterprise—can change our world. If even in the realm of religion, where division has run so deep for so long, a spirit of union can be forged, surely it must be possible to bring together citizens united by a common flag, and perhaps someday even by a common humanity.

But there are forces loosed in the land that would undermine this noble effort. In these pages, I have described what I once saw as an allergy to complexity and nuance, now a potentially toxic raging fever of secular dogmatism (similar in so many ways to the religious dogmatism of the Church of my youth), which poses a severe threat to the fabric of our society.

As President Obama put it: "Instead of our politics reflecting our values, we have politics infecting our communities." If those who care do not rise up now, it will be too late when they do.

I have argued that our universities, the engines of knowledge and stewards of thought, are our hope. Of course, they are threatened by the same forces that threaten society generally. But they also have the traditions and the structures not only to prevail against those forces, but to provide a model of dialogue and the expansion of knowledge that society could emulate.

What I have described as the global network university is an advanced form of a university committed at its core to providing an ecumenical model designed to broaden understanding through dialogue. The wonderful success of NYU Abu Dhabi and NYU Shanghai, intricately connected with each other and anchored by NYU New York in a worldwide circulatory system, proves that such universities are possible and attractive to very talented faculty and students. In the decades ahead, NYU and others who follow this model will modify it and improve upon it, as universities do with every idea.

If, as we hope, our universities provide the models that turn back the pervasive forces of secular dogmatism and foster the dialogic world of understanding we yearn to see, and if the integrative, ecumenical model of the global university becomes more common and proves capable of generating leaders committed to nourishing such a world, it will be all the more imperative that anyone who has the appetite and talent to thrive at our great universities be given the opportunity to attend them. This necessity, I have argued, requires aggressive efforts to discover talent that is likely to be overlooked, to ensure that students are matched with schools that fit their abilities, and to remove the financial obstacles that might prevent worthy students from attending a school that is best for them. Today, we tolerate a scandalous concentration of wealth; we must avoid a tomorrow in which we tolerate an even more scandalous concentration of hope and knowledge.

This is the sum of the argument I have made in this book and of my efforts over the years since Charlie called me to the vocation of teaching.

Some will say the world I have described is beyond reach, especially these days. But I have seen concrete results. I have seen a group of young women from a quite ordinary high school in Brooklyn commit themselves to mastering the tools of dialogue in competitive debate, and I have seen them do it so well that they would win five national championships.

I have seen dialogue, understanding, and love so permeate the Jewish and Muslim communities of NYU New York that they now regularly come together for joint service projects and gather as a joint religious community at a "Shabbat for 2,000."

I have seen first NYU Abu Dhabi and then NYU Shanghai knit together into vibrant communities students from literally every sector of every part of the world—students with as much talent as any school in the world, all under a banner of secular ecumenism.

And I have seen the faculty, students, administrators, and trustees of the largest private university in the world embrace a secular ecumenism as a mission and as their road to excellence.

●

As we look toward the future of civil society, we can choose nihilism or hope. I must choose hope—as an act of both faith and intellect.

After 9/11, there was an Axial moment available to us, and not just to us but to the world. We did not grasp it as we could have, for complex reasons, including divisions in American society precipitated and perpetuated by the march to war in Iraq and its aftermath.

And so, I believe it is not too late. In a wonderful piece first written for her students in the days just after 9/11 and later published in the *Wall Street Journal*, NYU's Joan Breton Connelly eloquently described the parallels between classical Athens and our New York after 9/11. In her beautiful words, written from a place deep within her spirit, she suggested what might be our future, if we make it so. In the years since, I often have reread her message of hope to lift my own spirits. I offer them now to those who have read my words in this book, in an effort to lift your spirits as well.

> In 480 B.C. the Persian army marched upon Athens and committed the unthinkable: the total destruction of the Acropolis. This devastation took place not on a field of battle but in the very heart of the city. The viciousness of the attack, directed at the venerable shrines held sacred by the Greeks, accomplished a sinister ambition. It tore down the very symbols of Greek culture and terrorized the civilians who watched helplessly.
>
> So stunned were the Greeks by this unspeakable act that they left the ruins untouched for more than 30 years. The site was to stand as a memorial lest anyone forget the atrocities committed upon Greek soil by this ruthless enemy.
>
> But in 447 B.C., under the leadership of the general and politician Pericles, Athens initiated a reconstruction program. From the cold ashes and debris were raised the gleaming white marble

buildings that stand to this day, manifestations of the very pinnacle of Greek art and architecture. The Parthenon, which has become a cultural icon embodying democracy itself, was, in fact, built as a replacement for the temples that had preceded it.

The long view from history is an invaluable source of hope. It was following tragedy that the Greeks achieved their finest moment. Along with the Parthenon came a full flourishing of art, literature, theater, philosophy, religion and politics, culminating in the development of the democratic system of government. The Athenians responded to outside threat by forging the new and utterly revolutionary concept of self-sacrifice for the common good. From this newly hewn bond of altruism, a strong communal identity was born, one of unity in the face of adversity.[1]

So it can be for our generation and those that follow. Out of the seeming dark spiral in which we find ourselves, even with its peril to society and to universities, we can seize an opportunity. It is time to call ourselves and society to a higher plane. And in a pluralistic civil society, that plane is what makes us distinctly human—the plane of the mind. In recent years, what we have seen is a marginalization of seriousness. What we need instead is a marginalization of dogmatism.

That realization brings the role of research universities to the fore. We need them to become a force and a model—to offer an alternative vision as well as a rebuke to the coliseum culture. We must marshal our academic and then our political leaders to press the agenda of true discourse, beginning with attention to the quality of conversation within our universities and then disseminating into American life the standards and habits of inquiry so central to our campuses at their best.

●

Let me close this work with a few very personal words.

In 1975, I left my position as chair of the religion department at Saint Francis College in Brooklyn and my wonderful life working with high school debaters for a new life at Harvard Law School. That move elevated my life—not just my resume, but my life.

The education I received at Harvard was important, of course; without it I would not be where I am today. But the real elevation came not from the education Harvard gave me but from the presence in my class of the most wonderful person I ever have met, Lisa Goldberg. We fell in love, were married within two months of holding hands for the first time, and for more than thirty years, we were more in love with each passing day.

Over a decade ago, on a January Sunday, she died. In an instant. No warning. We had enjoyed a lovely day together. Ironically or providentially, I spent a good part of it preparing a speech I was to deliver that week, a speech in which I was to discuss the spate of books by authors like Richard Dawkins and Samuel Harris that attacked a simple-minded view of an anthropomorphic God quite foreign to me and to millions of people of faith. As always, Lisa was helping me frame my thoughts. At 6:45, I checked to see if she wanted me to get dinner; she asked that I come back in about a half-hour, so that she could finish some reading she wanted to discuss with me. When I returned, she was gone. The last words we had said to each other as I left the room earlier were, "I love you." I cherish that exchange to this day.

In his wonderful book *A Grief Observed*, C. S. Lewis writes from his own grief at his wife's passing:

> For both lovers, and for all pairs of lovers without exception, bereavement is a universal and integral part of our experience of love. It follows marriage as normally as marriage follows courtship or as autumn follows summer. It is not a truncation of the process but one of its phases; not the interruption of the dance, but the next figure. We are 'taken out of ourselves' by the loved one while she is here. Then comes the tragic figure of the dance in which we must learn to be still taken out of ourselves though the bodily presence is withdrawn, to love the very Her, and not to fall back to loving our past, or our memory, or our sorrow, or our relief from sorrow, or our own love.

Today, we continue to dance. I try to live each day in a way that is worthy of Lisa's love and I work to represent adequately both of us in the corporeal world. She devoted her life, in ways far beyond my talents, to bringing together the estranged peoples of our nation and of the world and to empowering in that ecumenical world the voices and peoples traditionally absent from the conversation.

I may think of myself alone as Don Quixote, off tilting at windmills on a fool's errand. But I cannot think of Lisa that way, nor could anyone who knew her or who saw what she accomplished. So I am emboldened.

I tell my students, the wonderful carriers of talent and enthusiasm I see in my daily life, that they should not seek to "change the world"; instead, they should seek first to center themselves in the values they embrace, and then they should work outward (in the Confucian ever-expanding circles of human relatedness) to reinforce themselves by finding the right life partner, then to install their values in a loving family and group of friends. Only then can they gradually change their town, city, country, and the world.

Our nation and the world are under siege by those who would infect our society with a powerful dogmatism, their revealed secular truth. Surrender is not an option, for surrender yields nothing. No matter the odds, we must fight. Thankfully, in our universities, as they are and as they can be, we have a model of the society that could be. Let us begin by calling them to their values and developing in them genuinely mutual and ecumenical communities, truly available to all who have the gift and desire to participate. Then let us move out through ever-widening circles to imbue our societies with those values.

This is not a quixotic mission. It is a vital mission.

Onward and upward—together—to the Second Axial Age.

Notes

Preface

1. Saint Brendan's High School, a parochial school that went out of existence in 1980.

2. "Back to School: Older Students on the Rise in College Classrooms," NBC News, August 28, 2014, www.nbcnews.com/business/business-news/back-school-older-students-rise-college-classrooms-n191246.

1
Dogmatism, Complexity, and Civic Discourse

1. Dick Young, "Brooklyn Loses Dodgers to Los Angeles in 1957," *New York Daily News*, October 9, 1957, www.dailynews.com/sports/baseball/brooklyn-loses-dodgers-los-angeles-1957-article-1.2381894.

2. "Sharp Partisan Divisions in Views of National Institutions," People-Press .org, Pew Research Center, July 10, 2017, www.people-press.org/2017/07/10/sharp-partisan-divisions-in-views-of-national-institutions/2.

3. Pierre Teilhard de Chardin, *The Phenomenon of Man,* trans. Bernard Wall (New York: Harper Perennial Modern Thought, 2008).

4. Anthony Black, "The 'Axial Period': What Was It and What Does It Signify?" *Review of Politics* 70, no. 1 (Winter 2008), available at Simon Fraser University, www.sfu.ca/~poitras/rp_axial_08.pdf, 23–39.

5. Albert O. Hirschman, preface to *The Rhetoric of Reaction* (Cambridge, MA: Harvard University Press, 1991), x.

6. "Political Polarization in the American Public," People-Press.org, Pew Research Center, June 2014, www.people-press.org/2014/06/12/political-polarization-in-the-american-public.

7. Shanto Iyengar, Gaurav Sood, and Yphtach Lelkes, "Affect, Not Ideology: A Social Identity Perspective on Polarization," *Public Opinion Quarterly* 76, no. 3 (January 2012): 405–31.

8. "The Partisan Divide on Political Values Grows Even Wider," Pew Research Center, October 2017, http://assets.pewresearch.org/wp-content/uploads/sites/5/2017/10/05162647/10-05-2017-Political-landscape-release.pdf, 1.

9. Hanna Rosin, "Beyond Belief," *The Atlantic,* January–February 2005, www.theatlantic.com/magazine/archive/2005/01/beyond-belief/303667.

10. See John Sexton, "We Must Protect the Law and Its Role from the Demagogues," *Newsletter: Association of American Law Schools* (November 1997).

11. Ibid.

12. Michael Barthel and Amy Mitchell, "Americans' Attitude about the News Media Deeply Divided along Partisan Lines," Pew Research Center, May 2017, www.journalism.org/2017/05/10/americans-attitudes-about-the-news-media-deeply-divided-along-partisan-lines.

13. Corwin D. Smidt, "Polarization and the Decline of the American Floating Voter," *American Journal of Political Science* (October 2015), https://onlinelibrary.wiley.com/doi/epdf/10.1111/ajps.12218.

14. Richard Foley, *Working Without a Net: A Study of Egocentric Epistemology* (New York: Oxford University Press, 1993).

2

The Traditional University as Sacred Space for Discourse

1. *Fordham Alumni Magazine* (Summer 2004).

2. April Glaser, "Long before Snowden, Librarians Were Anti-Surveillance Heroes," *Slate* (June 2015), www.slate.com/blogs/future_tense/2015/06/03/usa_freedom_act_before_snowden_librarians_were_the_anti_surveillance_heroes.html.

3. Institute of International Education, "2004 IIE Annual Report" (2004), https://p.widencdn.net/s1d3yn/2004-IIE-Annual-Report.

4. Catherine Morris, "Open Doors 2017 Executive Summary," Institute of International Education, November 2017, https://www.iie.org/Why-IIE/Announcements/2017-11-13-Open-Doors-2017-Executive-Summary.

5. Nick Anderson, "Report Finds Fewer New International Students on U.S. College Campuses," *Washington Post*, November 13, 2017, www.washingtonpost.com/local/education/report-finds-fewer-new-international-students-on-us-college-campuses/2017/11/12/5933fe02-c61d-11e7-aae0-cb18a8c29c65_story.html?noredirect=on&utm_term=.c12683ba9ca7.

6. Elizabeth Redden, "Will U.S. Restrict Visas for Chinese Students?" Inside Higher Ed, March 16, 2018, www.insidehighered.com/news/2018/03/16/reports-trump-administration-considering-limits-visas-chinese-citizens-cause-concern.

7. Bethany Allen-Ebrahimian, "300,000 Chinese Students Attend U.S. Colleges. What Will They Learn About American Life?" *Foreign Policy* (October 2016), https://foreignpolicy.com/2016/10/07/300000-chinese-students-attend-u-s-colleges-what-will-they-learn-about-american-life-china-u-survey-backstory.

8. Elizabeth Redden, "Did Trump Call Most Chinese Students Spies?" Inside Higher Ed, August 9, 2018, www.insidehighered.com/news/2018/08/09/politico-reports-trump-called-most-chinese-students-us-spies.

9. Letter from Alan Goodman, sixth president of the Institute of International Education, to the Board of Trustees.

10. Michael Hiltzik, "Reduced Public Funding for Basic Research Leaves U.S. in the Scientific Dust," *Los Angeles Times*, April 28, 2015, www.latimes.com/business/hiltzik/la-fi-mh-the-funding-decline-in-basic-research-20150428-column.html.

11. R. F. Hamilton and L. L. Hargens, "The Politics of the Professors: Self-Identifications 1969–1984," *Social Forces* 71, no. 3 (1993): 603–27.

12. Neil Gross and Solon Simmons, "The Social and Political Views of American Professors," Conservative Criminology, September 2007, www.conservativecriminology.com/uploads/5/6/1/7/56173731/lounsbery_9-25.pdf, 59.

13. Ibid., 59.

14. Ibid., 60.

15. Michael Vasquez, "5 Takeaways from Turning Point's Plan to 'Commandeer' Campus Elections," *Chronicle of Higher Education* (April 2018), www.chronicle.com/article/5-Takeaways-From-Turning/243064.

16. Jon A. Shields and Joshua M. Dunn, Sr., *Passing on the Right: Conservative Professors in the Progressive University* (New York: Oxford University Press, 2016), 60.

17. Stephen L. Carter, *Civility: Manners, Morals, and the Etiquette of Democracy* (New York: HarperPerennial, 1999).

18. Mark Sherman, "As Others See Us," *Psychology Today* (December 2013), www.psychologytoday.com/us/blog/real-men-dont-write-blogs/201312/others-see-us.

19. John Sexton, introductory speech to a university-wide forum, New York University, New York, 2015.

20. "fire's 2017 Year in Review for Student and Faculty Rights on Campus," Foundation for Individual Rights in Education, December 28, 2017, www.thefire.org/fires-2017-year-in-review-for-student-and-faculty-rights-on-campus.

21. "About Us," Heterodox Academy, n.d., https://heterodoxacademy.org/about-us.

22. "FAQs," Heterodox Academy, n.d., https://heterodoxacademy.org/about-us/faqs.

23. Lorelle L. Espinosa, Jennifer R. Crandall, and Philip Wilkinson, "Free Speech and Campus Inclusion: A Survey of College Presidents," Higher Education Today, April 9, 2018, www.higheredtoday.org/2018/04/09/free-speech-campus-inclusion-survey-college-presidents/, 69.

24. Emily Mace, "Eliot, Charles W. (1834–1926)," Harvard Square Library, March 29, 2014, www.harvardsquarelibrary.org/biographies/charles-w-eliot-harvard-university-president.

25. See Jonathan King, "Chancellor Berdahl Speaks Out on U.S. Foreign Policy," UC Berkeley News, March 18, 2003, www.berkeley.edu/news/media/releases/2003/03/18_berdahl-war.shtml.

26. Ibid.

27. "University of Florida Estimates $600,000 Being Spent on Alt-Right Event Security," ABC 13, October 2017, http://abc13.com/politics/uf-says-it-is-paying-high-price-for-spencer-speech/2550945/.

28. Inside Higher Ed, "Survey of College and University Admission Directors," 2017, www.insidehighered.com/booklet/2017-survey-college-and-university-admissions-directors, 80.

29. William J. Stuntz, "Church and University: Maybe It's Time for the Enterprises to Join Hands," SF Gate, January 9, 2005, www.sfgate.com/opinion/article/Church-and-university-Maybe-it-s-time-for-the-2740271.php.

30. McDaniel v. Paty, 435 U.S. 618 (1978).

3

A University for an Ecumenical World

1. Karl Jaspers, The Origin and Goal of History, trans. Michael Bullock (New Haven: Yale University Press, 1953).

2. Pierre Teilhard de Chardin, The Phenomenon of Man, trans. Bernard Wall (London: Fontana/Collins, 1965), 262.

3. Ewert H. Cousins, Christ of the 21st Century (New York: Continuum, 1998).

4. "Prime Minister Gordon Brown Delivers Foreign Policy Address at Kennedy Library," John F. Kennedy Presidential Library and Museum, Summer 2008, www.jfklibrary.org/About-Us/JFK-Library-Foundation/~/media/8812B42C96F04EBFB0B5C021549062C5.pdf.

5. Ibid.

6. Bruce Lambert, "40 Percent in New York Born Abroad," *New York Times*, July 24, 2000, www.nytimes.com/2000/07/24/nyregion/40-percent-in-new-york-born-abroad.html.

7. "Total and Foreign-born Population New York City, 1790–2000," New York City Department of City Planning Population Division, www1.nyc.gov/assets/planning/download/pdf/data-maps/nyc-population/historical-population/1790-2000_nyc_total_foreign_birth.pdf.

8. New York City Department of Planning, *Employment Patterns in New York City: Trends in a Growing Economy*, Official Web Site of the City of New York, July 2016, https://www1.nyc.gov/assets/planning/download/pdf/data-maps/nyc-economy/employment-patterns-nyc.pdf.

9. New York State Office of Higher Education, "Statewide Plan for Higher Education, 2004–2012," www.highered.nysed.gov/swp/page7.htm.

10. Commission on Independent Colleges and Universities in New York, *Talent Magnet: New York's Independent Sector Attracts Students from across the United States*, based on statistics from the National Center for Education Statistics, Integrated Postsecondary Education Data System, https://www.cicu.org/publications-research/matter-fact/talent-magnet-new-yorks-independent-sector-attracts-students-across-united-states.

11. "*US News and World Report* Annual Rankings," *US News and World Report*, 2018, www.usnews.com/best-graduate-schools/top-medical-schools/research-rankings.

12. Kwame Anthony Appiah, "Cosmopolitan Patriots," *Critical Inquiry* 23, no. 3 (Spring 1997), www-jstor-org.proxy.library.nyu.edu/stable/pdf/1344038.pdf?refreqid=excelsior%3Ad246554661b23ce406afbc45f443556f, 617–39.

13. Ibid., 618.

14. Jamil Salmi, "From Zero to Hero: Building World-Class Universities," World University Rankings, May 31, 2012, www.timeshighereducation.com/world-university-rankings/2012/one-hundred-under-fifty/analysis/world-class-university.

15. Global Higher Ed, "University Viewpoint: The University of Warwick on 'The Challenge of Global Education and Research,'" November 6, 2007, globalhighered.wordpress.com/2007/11/06/university-viewpoint-university-of-warwick.

16. Letter to the Yale community from President Richard C. Levin and Provost Peter Salovey, March 30, 2011, referenced in "NUS and Yale to Create Singapore's First Liberal Arts College," *Yale News*, March 31, 2011, https://news.yale.edu/2011/03/31/nus-and-yale-create-singapore-s-first-liberal-arts-college.

17. John Endicott, "Globalization: Its Meaning in an Educational Context," *Korea Herald*, March 2010, www.koreaherald.com/view.php?ud=20100323000377.

18. American Council on Education, *Strength through Global Leadership and Engagement: U.S. Higher Education in the 21st Century,* November 2011, www.acenet.edu/news-room/Documents/2011-CIGE-BRPReport.pdf.

19. Jonathan Sacks, "The Dignity of Difference: How to Avoid the Clash of Civilizations," *Sacred Heart University Review* 25, no. 1, art. 2 (2008).

20. Mohamad Bazzi, "N.Y.U. in Abu Dhabi: A Sectarian Bargain," *New York Times,* September 26, 2017, https://www.nytimes.com/2017/09/26/opinion/nyu-abu-dhabi.html.

21. Ibid.

22. New York University, "Exchange of Letters on Global Mobility at NYU Abu Dhabi (Faculty Committee on the Global Network)," January 2018, www.nyu.edu/about/leadership-university-administration/office-of-the-president/communications/exchange-of-letters-on-global-mobility-at-nyu-abu-dhabi-faculty-committee.html.

23. Ariel Kaminer, "Workers at NYU's Abu Dhabi Site Faced Harsh Conditions," *New York Times,* May 19, 2014, www.nytimes.com/2014/05/19/nyregion/workers-at-nyus-abu-dhabi-site-face-harsh-conditions.html?hp.

24. Nardello & Co., *Report of the Independent Investigator into Allegations of Labor and Compliance Issues during the Contruction of the NYU Abu Dhabi Campus on Saadiyat Island, United Arab Emirates,* April 2015, www.nardelloandco.com/wp-content/uploads/information/nyu-abu-dhabi-campus-investigative-report.pdf.

25. Ibid., 13.

26. Impact Ltd., *External Labor Compliance Monitoring at NYUAD Report,* May 2018, https://nyuad.nyu.edu/content/dam/nyuad/about/social-responsibility/compliance-monitoring-at-nyuad-report-may-2018.pdf.

27. Rima Al Mokarrab, Presidential Medal acceptance address, speech at graduation ceremony, Abu Dhabi, May 2015.

28. *Board of Education v. Allen,* 392 U.S. 236 (1968).

4

The Final Ingredient

1. Camille L. Ryan and Kurt Bauman "Educational Attainment in the United States: 2015," U.S. Census Bureau, March 2016, www.census.gov/content/dam/Census/library/publications/2016/demo/p20-578.pdf. For international data, see: "Education at a Glance 2017: OECD Indicators," OECD Library, September 2017, http://dx.doi.org/10.1787/eag-2017-en.

2. John Henry Cardinal Newman, *The Idea of a University* (London: Longmans, Green, 1893).

3. Jaroslav Pelikan, *The Idea of the University: A Reexamination* (New Haven: Yale University Press, 1992), 162.

4. Jake Bryant and Jimmy Sarakatsannis, "Why US Education Is Ready for Investment," McKinsey and Company, July 2015, www.mckinsey.com/industries/social-sector/our-insights/why-us-education-is-ready-for-investment, 163.

5. Christina Theokas and Marni Bromberg, "Falling Out of the Lead: Following High Achievers through High School and Beyond," Education Trust, April 2, 2014, https://edtrust.org/resource/falling-out-of-the-lead-following-high-achievers-through-high-school-and-beyond.

6. William G. Bowen, Matthew M. Chingos, and Michael S. McPherson, *Crossing the Finish Line: Completing College at America's Public Universities* (Princeton, NJ: Princeton University Press, 2009).

7. Chungseo Kang and Darlene Garcia Torres, "Study Snapshot: College Undermatching, Degree Attainment, and Minority Students," American Educational Research Association, April 2018, www.aera.net/Study-Snapshot-College-Undermatching-Degree-Attainment-and-Minority-Students.

8. "School Quality," NYC Department of Education, 2018, https://www.schools.nyc.gov/about-us/reports/school-quality.

9. "Our Results," College Advising Corps, https://advisingcorps.org/our-impact/our-results/.

10. "Our Results," College Advising Corps, https://advisingcorps.org/our-impact/our-results/.

11. Ibid.

12. Robert B. Archibald and David Feldman, *Why Does College Cost So Much?* (New York: Oxford University Press, 2011).

13. Robert B. Archibald and David Feldman, "The Anatomy of College Tuition," American Council on Education, April 2012, www.acenet.edu/news-room/Documents/Anatomy-of-College-Tuition.pdf.

14. Christopher S. Rugaber, "Pay Gap between College Grads and Everyone Else at a Record," *USA Today*, January 12, 2017, www.usatoday.com/story/money/2017/01/12/pay-gap-between-college-grads-and-everyone-else-record/96493348.

15. College Board, "Trends in Higher Education: Tuition and Fees and Room and Board over Time," 2018, https://trends.collegeboard.org/college-pricing/figures-tables/tuition-fees-room-and-board-over-time.

16. College Board, "Trends in Higher Education: Average Net Price over Time for Full-Time Students, by Sector," 2017, https://trends.collegeboard.org/college-pricing/figures-tables/average-net-price-over-time-full-time-students-sector.

17. Ibid.

18. Meta Brown et al., "Looking at Student Loan Defaults through a Larger Window," Liberty Street Economics, Federal Reserve Bank of New York, February 19, 2015, http://libertystreeteconomics.newyorkfed.org/2015/02/looking_at_student_loan_defaults_through_a_larger_window.html.

19. Sandy Baum, Student Debt: Rhetoric and Realities of Higher Education Financing (New York: Palgrave Macmillan, 2016); Beth Akers and Matthew M. Chingos, Game of Loans: The Rhetoric and Reality of Student Debt (Princeton, NJ: Princeton University Press, 2016).

20. Stephanie Riegg Cellini "Gainfully Employed? New Evidence on the Earnings, Employment, and Debt of for-Profit Certificate Students," Brookings Institution, February 2018, www.brookings.edu/blog/brown-center-chalkboard/2018/02/09/gainfully-employed-new-evidence-on-the-earnings-employment-and-debt-of-for-profit-certificate-students.

21. David Autor, "Skills, Education, and the Rise of Earnings Inequality among the 'Other 99 Percent,'" Science, May 2014, http://science.sciencemag.org/content/344/6186/843.

22. Gallup, Great Jobs Great Lives: The 2014 Gallup-Purdue Index Report; A Study of More Than 30,000 College Graduates across the U.S., 2014, Purdue University, www.gallup.com/file/services/176768/GallupPurdueIndex_Report_2014.pdf.

23. Beth Akers, "Reconsidering the Conventional Wisdom on Student Loan Debt and Home Ownership," Brookings Institution, May 2014, www.brookings.edu/research/reconsidering-the-conventional-wisdom-on-student-loan-debt-and-home-ownership.

24. Stephen Burd, "Moving On Up? What a Ground Breaking Study Tells Us about Access, Success, and Mobility in Higher Ed," New America Foundation, October 2017, www.newamerica.org/education-policy/policy-papers/moving-on-up-series.

25. Christy Rakoczy, "Pay as You Earn (PAYE): How It Works, How to Qualify," Student Loan Hero, March 2018, www.studentloanhero.com/student-loans/student-loan-repayment/pay-as-you-earn-guide.

26. Ibid.

27. Governor Andrew M. Cuomo, "2015 Opportunity Agenda: Restoring Economic Opportunity," January 18, 2015, New York State, www.governor.ny.gov/news/2015-opportunity-agenda-restoring-economic-opportunity-2.

28. Federal Student Aid, "Federal Student Loan Portfolio," U.S. Department of Education, n.d., https://studentaid.ed.gov/sa/about/data-center/student/portfolio.

29. David Jesse, "Government Books $41.3 Billion in Student Loan Profits," USA Today, November 25, 2013, www.usatoday.com/story/news/nation/2013/11/25/federal-student-loan-profit/3696009.

30. Congressional Budget Office, "H.R. 4508, Promoting Real Opportunity, Success, and Prosperity through Education Reform Act," February 6, 2018, www.cbo.gov/publication/53547.

31. David L. Kirp, *Shakespeare, Einstein, and the Bottom Line: The Marketing of Higher Education* (Cambridge, MA: Harvard University Press, 2004).

32. Kate Redman, "263 Million Children And Youth Are Out of School from Primary to Upper Secondary," Global Education Monitoring Report, UNESCO, https://en.unesco.org/gem-report/sites/gem-report/files/OOSC_press_release.pdf.

33. UNHCR, the UN Refugee Agency, *Global Trends: Forced Displacement in 2017*, 2017, www.unhcr.org/5b27be547.pdf.

34. Relief Web, "Turkey Reveals How 660,000 Syrian Refugee Children Will Move into State Schools," September 2007, https://theirworld.org/news/turkey-plan-will-get-all-syrian-refugee-children-in-school.

35. Elizabeth Redden, "The Refugee Crisis and Higher Ed," Inside Higher Ed, September 25, 2015, www.insidehighered.com/news/2015/09/25/syrian-refugee-crisis-and-higher-education.

36. Jeff Daniels, "Navy's 'Significant Bet' on a $13B Supercarrier Dogged as an Expensive Boondoggle While Threats Loom," CNBC, July 2017, www.cnbc.com/2017/07/22/ford-carrier-emblematic-of-navys-struggle-with-technology-costs.html.

Conclusion

1. Joan Breton Connelly, "The Athenian Response to Terror," *Wall Street Journal*, February 19, 2002, www.wsj.com/articles/SB1014086321226175240.

Acknowledgments

I am grateful to all the colleagues who have helped me shape the views contained in these pages. And I am grateful as well to my students, who for six decades have added so much to my life.

Important work on the manuscript was done during my time as the Kluge Distinguished Professor at the Library of Congress (2016); I thank my colleague and friend Jane McAuliffe for making that possible.

In particular, I must thank the dear friends who took time to read various drafts of this work and whose comments improved this book and sharpened my thinking: Rima Al Mokarab, Bob Berne, Lynne Brown, Arthur Browne, Jim Carroll, Jules Coleman, Jamie Deutsch, Dick Foley, Terry Hartle, Ron Herzman, Jonathan Sacks, Ellen Schall, and James Traub.

Joe Conason and Nessa Rapoport deserve special mention: They spent days over a year pacing me through the development of each draft and contributing to it at every turn.

I am deeply indebted to Gordon Brown, former Prime Minister of the United Kingdom, my hero and cherished friend, for his generosity to me in life and for the wonderful foreword he has written.

And special thanks to Bob Berdahl, the president's president and my brother in arms, who nurtured my faith in this project from the beginning, and who has written an incisive foreword for the Chinese edition.

Most of all, love and thanks to the wonderful family that sustains me and inspires me to believe in the possibility of a world filled with love: my spectacular granddaughters, Julia, Ava, and Natalie; my son, Jed, and his bride of twenty years, Danielle; my daughter, Katie; and Lisa, who created our collective world and who guides us to be better each day.

Index